"What do you call a book that rattles our comfortable certainties while somehow leaving us sturdier and more joyful, a book that dances in the mysteries without going mushy or cynical, a book that stubbornly insists we find God in the kitchen as much as the cloister? I call this book a paradox. I call it a wonder."
Winn Collier, author of *Holy Curiosity*

"A book that celebrates the glorious 'and' (not 'or') of Christian spirituality, *Surprised by Paradox* has many ands of its own: it is accessible and smart, relatable and challenging, a page-turner and theologically profound. With clarity and richness, Jen Pollock Michel invites us to sit before the beautiful mystery of God without resisting, diminishing, or seeking to solve or untangle it, which is to say, she invites us into the depths of worship."
Tish Harrison Warren, author of *Liturgy of the Ordinary*

"So much of the beauty of Christianity is in its paradoxes, the marvelous mysteries that form the center of our faith: the Word made flesh, God become human, law fulfilled by grace, death conquered by death once and for all. With beauty and elegance, Jen Pollock Michel reveals and revels in the mysteries of a faith that cannot be contained by human categories or understanding but beckons us to embrace its certainties and its wonders alike."
Karen Swallow Prior, author of *On Reading Well* and *Fierce Convictions*

"What is the shape of the kingdom of God? And how can we find our fit? Jen Pollock Michel submits that it's only by embracing paradox—a God who is both king and baby, strong and vulnerable, and who says dying is the only way to live. With insightful clarity, Jen highlights our call to a faith that invites us to form a sacred, expectant circle around one tiny word—*and*. No matter how hard we may try to ease the tension of the kingdom life, this book is a subversive invitation to make peace with the paradoxical way of Jesus."
Emily P. Freeman, author of *Simply Tuesday* and *The Next Right Thing*

"There is no one else I would rather see write a book on paradox than Jen Pollock Michel. Her writing is full of tension, cadence, wisdom, and beauty. She is a rare gift to the world of Christian publishing and *Surprised by Paradox* is unsurprisingly worthy of her writing and wisdom. She carefully draws out her readers while drawing them into the greater narrative of Scripture and God himself, showing us faith is in its nature, strange, surprising, and unequivocally beautiful. Each one of Jen's books becomes my favorite of hers and this one surpassed them all."
Lore Ferguson Wilbert, author of *Handle with Care*

"In a world of *us* and *them*, the logical solution to every question must be *this* or *that*. Either you can believe, embrace, hold, and affirm *this*, or you can believe, embrace, hold, and affirm *that*. In *Surprised by Paradox*, Jen Pollock Michel calls us above these limited categories, directing us to the mystery of the *both . . . and*. But do not confuse this as a call for the mushy middle or even finding common ground. No, paradox does not let us escape so easily and is only satisfied when our eyes look beyond this earth in wonder of the Divine."

Hannah Anderson, author of *All That's Good: Recovering the Lost Art of Discernment*

"This book is wise and compelling. Jen Pollock Michel does what any good Bible scholar worth his or her salt does—examines the whole of Scripture, not just pet passages or doctrines. In doing so, Michel demonstrates that when it comes to God's kingdom, honesty requires we befriend paradox and the tension in the *and* instead of taking an immovable *either/or* stance. Does that mean anything goes, that truth is relative? Quite the contrary. If anything, Michel is thoroughly orthodox. She is one of the foremost public evangelical theologians and Bible teachers of our time. I for one look to her for wisdom."

Marlena Graves, author of *A Beautiful Disaster: Finding Hope in the Midst of Brokenness*

"Oversimplifications are dangerous. Especially in theology and public life we need and rely on people who are capable of living into the challenging paradoxes we find in the Gospels. Rich with personal stories and reflections, Michel's explorations of what it means to live by 'both-and' rather than 'either-or' offer a vision of Christian hospitality without laxity and theological integrity without rigidity. This is a timely, practical, and thought-provoking book."

Marilyn McEntyre, author of *Caring for Words in a Culture of Lies, Word by Word,* and *Make a List*

SURPRISED
by
PARA
DOX

THE PROMISE
of And in an
EITHER-OR WORLD

JEN POLLOCK MICHEL
Foreword by Russ Ramsey

IVP Books

An imprint of InterVarsity Press
Downers Grove, Illinois

InterVarsity Press
P.O. Box 1400, Downers Grove, IL 60515-1426
ivpress.com
email@ivpress.com

InterVarsity Press® is the book-publishing division of InterVarsity Christian Fellowship/USA®, a movement of students and faculty active on campus at hundreds of universities, colleges, and schools of nursing in the United States of America, and a member movement of the International Fellowship of Evangelical Students. For information about local and regional activities, visit intervarsity.org.

Scripture quotations, unless otherwise noted, are from The Holy Bible, English Standard Version, copyright © 2001 by Crossway Bibles, a division of Good News Publishers. Used by permission. All rights reserved.

While any stories in this book are true, some names and identifying information may have been changed to protect the privacy of individuals.

Cover design: David Fassett
Interior design: Daniel van Loon
Images: trees in forest: © Alexander Schitschka / EyeEm / Getty Images
white textured wall: © Nadine Westveer / EyeEm / Getty Images
forest of trees: © Laura Frediani / EyeEm / Getty Images
flock of flying birds: © Amir Mukhtar / Moment collection / Getty Images

ISBN 978-0-8308-4564-4 (print)
ISBN 978-0-8308-7092-9 (digital)

Printed in the United States of America ∞

InterVarsity Press is committed to ecological stewardship and to the conservation of natural resources in all our operations. This book was printed using sustainably sourced paper.

Library of Congress Cataloging-in-Publication Data
A catalog record for this book is available from the Library of Congress.

P	21	20	19	18	17	16	15	14	13	12	11	10	9	8	7	6	5	4	3	2	1
Y	37	36	35	34	33	32	31	30	29	28	27	26	25	24	23	22	21	20	19		

To Jonas McAnn and the pastors like him.

Thank you for preaching the truth and

trying not to miss the wonder.

We have heard the fact. Let us seek the mystery.

AUGUSTINE

CONTENTS

FOREWORD

Russ Ramsey

*The kingdom of God is as if a man should scatter seed on
the ground. He sleeps and rises night and day, and the
seed sprouts and grows; he knows not how.*

MARK 4:26-27

When I was in my early twenties, I discovered the joy of studying theology. I found myself aligning with a large number of other people like me who were discovering a theological framework for understanding God and the world that seemed watertight.

As a young man interested in ministry and theology, I marveled at the way the doctrines I was learning made God, the world, and my place in it fit together like a puzzle. Putting the puzzle together took work, but the promise was that if I kept at it, I would come to see the things of God with a kind of crystal clarity that would make my faith, and my calling, unassailable.

That was half my life ago. I still love studying theology, and I have not abandoned the doctrines that took hold of my heart and mind when I was younger. But many of the ideas about God I assumed would have become crystal clear to me at this point in my life seem to have withdrawn more into the shadows of mystery—remaining ever-present while managing to evade capture. The older I get, the more I discover that certainty can be elusive.

I want to be clear here. I believe in certainty, but I do not believe in comprehensive certainty. Anyone who says they do is either a liar or a fool. We don't know what we don't know. The apostle Paul wrote, "Now we see in a mirror dimly, but then face to face. Now I know in part; then I shall know fully, even as I have been fully known" (1 Cor 13:12).

We know in part.

In terms of the essentials of saving faith, God's word is clear. He gave us Scripture "so that you may believe that Jesus is the Christ, the Son of God, and that by believing you may have life in his name" (Jn 20:31). God's word is "able to make you wise for salvation through faith in Christ Jesus" (2 Tim 3:15).

And yet, here lies a paradox. Even of the things we're certain about, we only know in part. For example, I know that "Christ Jesus is the one who died—more than that, who was raised—who is at the right hand of God, who indeed is interceding for us" (Rom 8:34). But please don't ask me to describe that room or recite Christ's prayer. Even my best guess would fall way short.

Seeing through the glass dimly is not a flaw in the system. Rather, it is in keeping with what we know about God. God is glorious. Moses only saw the back part of a passing God, and that while hidden in the cleft of a rock, because if he saw any more, he would have died (see Ex 33:20-23). Mystery abounds when dealing with God because he is God and we are not. Allowing for paradox does not represent a weakened approach to theological understanding. On the contrary, it allows for a robust theology, one that is filled with the sort of awe that not only regards God as unimaginably wondrous but also awakens in us the same desire Moses had to see him as he is.

Theological understanding should not become a substitute for faith. Studied rightly, theology should lead to awe and wonder. To that end, my friend Jen Pollock Michel has given us a gift. It seems to me that the church has a renewed appetite for wonder, mystery, paradox, and awe, so *Surprised by Paradox* comes at an important time.

As a pastor, I have seen the danger that comes with believing God can be solved like an equation. When we treat him like a system of theological points rather than the glorious Creator of heaven and earth, we end up bending what we think about him to fit the structure we think contains him. The problem with this is that my twenty-year-old understanding of God doesn't fit into the box the God I know now in my forties requires. And I have to believe that if I reach my seventies, my view of him will be different in many ways from what it is today.

I am not talking about abandoning orthodoxy or venturing away from the faith. God forbid. I am talking about venturing deeper in. Today, my understanding of God is informed by suffering, vocational challenges, parental struggles, and a deeper understanding of my own sin that were not in play in my twenties. My questions about God increase in number not because I know less, but because I know more. And as my questions increase, so does my faith, which Scripture esteems as a higher prize than certainty (see 1 Cor 13:13).

Jen describes *Surprised by Paradox* as "a book about faith in its lived-in condition—as it abides complexity rather than resists it." Surely abiding complexity rather than resisting it is a spiritual discipline. This book is a Biblically grounded, theologically sound guide for honing that skill. I am so glad she wrote it and that you are reading it.

Our culture races to the logical fallacy that says if something doesn't make sense to me, it must not make sense at all. What a tragically small view of the world folded into an even more tragically large view of ourselves. We were made to wonder, to form questions in our hearts that no other human being can answer— questions that belong to a world that transcends what we can comprehend. These questions do not drive us away from God; they draw us near.

Jesus said the seed sprouts and grows, and we know not how. In these pages, Jen Pollock Michel reminds us that though we know not how, the seeds still do sprout and grow. This is God's work. To wonder about such things is to worship. To God be the glory.

INTRODUCTION

A Little Bit of Wondering

*M*acey was good at cleaning my house. She was also good at proselytizing. She would search articles from the Jehovah's Witness website, then leave her phone on my desk as I worked on drafts of this book. "Read this," she would insist, wagging her finger before leaving to strip beds.

Macey, a housekeeper I'd hired from a Craigslist ad, had been studying six years to be baptized as a Jehovah's Witness, a movement that began with a small group of Bible students living near Pittsburgh, Pennsylvania, at the end of the nineteenth century when they undertook "a systematic analysis of the Bible." Comparing the doctrines taught by evangelical churches with the teachings of Scripture, they purportedly found great incongruity. "They began publishing their learning in books, newspapers, and the journal that is now called *The Watchtower—Announcing Jehovah's Kingdom.*"[1]

It was these systematic teachings of the Jehovah's Witnesses that Macey liked to share with me in long stretches of the afternoon. "I love Jehovah," she would exclaim as my thoughts drifted impatiently to the work that both of us were neglecting. I couldn't help believing her. But one afternoon burned with unusual intensity, even if Macey was hard of hearing and our communication halting. We scribbled furiously on Post-it Notes. We opened heavy tomes from my bookshelves. We parsed out meanings of Hebrew and Greek words.

Yet on this afternoon and every other, theology was a suburban cul-de-sac to circle endlessly. We never managed to get anywhere. In these afternoon conversations, Macey dogged me with difficult questions, and to be honest, despite having the résumé I do, I was short on answers.

As I began to understand it, the crusade for "orthodoxy" by the Jehovah's Witnesses had been a campaign to eliminate all the paradoxes of the Christian faith.

The paradox of the three-in-one God.

The paradox of the incarnation.

The paradox of grace.

The Jehovah's Witnesses seemed to have tidied faith like one might have straightened a drawer. They had tamed the roaring lion of doctrinal complexity by injuring one of its legs. Jesus was God—but not as fully god as Jehovah. (The Holy Spirit was simply an impersonal force of God's will.) God loved his people—but his people were still expected to prove themselves loveable. As Macey held her faith up for view, I saw right angles, straight lines, closed circles. It was the geometry of certainty, defended by proof.

"Mysteries," I wanted to call these paradoxes, even if the explanation felt a little like drawing my theological tail between my legs. Macey surely counted a mysterious faith to be an unreliable one.

She had neat rows, taut threads, and knotted ends. I had tangles. It's the tangles that are the concern of this book—the places of paradox in Christian faith, where we are obliged to uphold truths "logically at variance with one another."[2] My interest is in the crooked lines, the irregular shapes, the open circles—which is to say, not the proofs but the problems. Admittedly, the tangles are for many of us a source of confusion, fear, or chagrin. Whether when we find ourselves in conversation with a Jehovah's Witness or a person with no claim to religious faith, as evangelicals we'd much rather offer certainties to the world than questions. It's from our bastion of impregnable dogma that we feel safest.

▲ ● ■

In its best light, religious faith in Toronto, where I live, is considered a quaint artifact from earlier generations, much like the lace doilies our grandmothers used to adorn their furniture. Those doilies were never of much use, even if they were once considered beautiful. In its worst light, religious faith in Toronto is thought primitive and bigoted, the violent weapon of dogmatism in an enlightened, tolerant world. I expect the tangles to do damage to people like my agnostic Jewish friend, Shane, who has been reading the book of Numbers. I wonder, Will he feel, as Macey does, that the paradoxes of faith make a reasonable case for dismissing it? I wonder about my own responsibility for straightening the tangles for people like Ruben and Olga, my Russian neighbors across the street whose first understanding of Christ's resurrection came over a glass of wine in our kitchen. To my friends and my neighbors, I want to confidently make a defense of my hope when people ask; I'm just no longer sure that hope holds the same shape as certitude. Can't I sometimes say, "I don't know," or, "I'm not sure"?

I certainly grew up in a tradition with a lot of faith in the Bible to predict and answer every question. In the Southern Baptist churches I attended throughout my childhood, our pastors bent over their wooden pulpits with fervor, Sunday after Sunday, leaning on one hand to feverishly gesticulate with the other. The sermons were alliterated, every point as solid as the brass plate we passed during the offering. We tightened the belt of faith with Scriptures we memorized; we brandished the sword of truth with brazen self-assurance. I grew to love the Bible in those pews, grew hungry for every word that precedes from the mouth of God, grew up confidently believing that if bushes burned, God would surely tell us how and why.

> **The Bible was to be trusted for its encyclopedic knowledge; doubt signaled the failure to have read and understood it. Believers always needed more certainty, not less.**

The Bible was to be trusted for its encyclopedic knowledge; doubt signaled the failure to have read and understood it.

Believers always needed more certainty, not less.

Yet even as a sixteen-year-old, new to the daily practice of reading Scripture, I remember diving into the book of Revelation and surfacing from its murky waters with more curiosities than certainties. I was one of the lonely ones who turned the pages of Scriptures and turned up more wondering. I did not come to the easy compliance that others in my church seemed to muster, which is one way of saying that I saw less acquiescence in biblical faith and far more audacity.

In the pages of Scripture I found Abraham, who seemed to wonder irreverently about God's promises: "O Lord God, what will you give me, for I continue childless, and the heir of my house is Eliezer of Damascus?" I met Jacob, who tried striking a bargain with God at Bethel: "If God will be with me and will keep me in this way that I go, and will give me bread to eat and clothing to wear, so that I come again to my father's house in peace, then the LORD shall be my God." I encountered Moses, who doubted his ability to fulfill God's call and tried refusing the divine commission. "Oh, my Lord, please send someone else." I met Naomi, who blamed the Lord for her misfortunes: "I went away full, and the LORD has brought me back empty." I found Hannah, whose desperate prayers mimicked drunkenness: "Give to your servant a son."

In Scripture, I saw paradoxical qualities of faith that weren't commended to me from the pulpit: wondering, resisting, interrogating. In holy writ, I saw faith riddled with fallibility and fear. I saw the heroes of Scripture as emphatically human, getting a lot wrong even as they tried mustering some praise.

I started to wonder if tangles—and tangled faith—were less exception and more rule.

▲ ● ■

The Atlantic recently published a compilation of studies titled "Awesomeness Is Everything." In each of the studies, experts measured the effects of awe. As psychologists have described it, awe is "the experience of encountering something so vast—in size, skill, beauty, intensity, etc.—that we struggle to comprehend it and may even adjust our world to accommodate it."[3] Awe is our slack-jawed response to natural phenomena like waterfalls and childbirth. To feel awe is to confirm a beautiful, wild universe, a world we neither made nor control.

According to these scientific studies, when we feel awe, there are two characteristic effects. For the more agnostic among us, awe nurtures the belief "in evolution as an orderly versus random process." We may not credit a Creator for the beauty and bigness of natural phenomena, but neither will we dismiss them as completely accidental. For all the wildness of the world, we reckon it to be purposefully so. For those of us inclined to religious belief, awe nurtures our certainty about God. When we experience magnificence, it confirms our belief in a Maker. We understand nothing more purposeful than the divine hand carving out the mountains and crafting the human body.

The religious and irreligious alike experience awe. One looks more like worship, of course, but both are characterized, as the studies conclude, by the appetite for imposing order. In other words, in the world today we accept awesomeness, but we want it tamed. There is only so much mystery we can tolerate, only so much smallness we can assume.

To trace it historically, the appetite for order is a craving we've inherited from our Enlightenment fathers. Before the "flat" world of mystery had yet to be ironically flattened by modern hubris, the world was once considered to be an enchanted world, inhabited and acted on by invisible, spiritual forces.[4] As we were vulnerable to those forces (the boundary between the world and the self being porous and penetrable), we were never completely safe apart from the counterdefense that was God, mysteriously and materially present in the communion Host. Fear made heresy impossible—a menace to whole communities.

Then came Renaissance humanism, the scientific revolution, even the Reformation: the "sacramental tapestry" of the world—

this idea that the world could show us something of the transcendent, even God himself—was cut.[5] Mystery was expelled from the universe, and we were left with a "visible, measurable, and scientifically verifiable world," ready to be sliced open and splayed out.[6] Even the sacraments came to be understood differently: we met God not in the physical wafer and wine, but in the *representation* of his body and blood. Modernity gave us more certainty than uncertainty—or at the very least certainty *in* certainty. We've come to an unassailable confidence that mystery, by dint of inquiry and scientific effort, can be wrestled and pinned down and made to cry uncle. We are no longer victims of the unknowable: we are masters of our own understanding. The great modern lie is one of infinite human autonomy and control.

This shift of modernity—from an embrace of mystery to a rejection of it—has undoubtedly affected our approach to faith. Though the Bible has not changed, our reading of it has. It's confidence we now prize in life with God; uncertainty we resist. We don't accommodate mystery as well as our ancient and medieval forbearers, especially in theology. "Theology has suffered—among evangelicals as well as elsewhere—from an undue desire for clarity and control," writes theologian Hans Boersma.[7] We like our truth catalogued and ordered and systematized.

The Enlightenment's turn toward rationality makes us chafe in places of paradox. How can two seemingly contradictory principles be simultaneously true? It's one reason we will work so persistently to unknot the tangles. It's not simply that Macey or Shane reject a mysterious, paradoxical faith: I too can be made to disbelieve when I'm asked to abide complexity, dissonance, and contradiction in order to hold things in tension. We don't like faith acting like predicament.

Though we might acknowledge God as standing at the thunderous, tempestuous center of faith, we also want the waters still and glassy around him. But it is an old sin seduced by an old lie that we can be like God, perfectly knowing as he knows.

Paradox has promise for forming humility in us all.

A book about paradox is a book about spiritual posture: the posture of kneeling under God's great big sky and admitting that mystery is inherent to the nature of God. As soon as we think we have God figured out, we will have ceased to worship him as he is. God, in his very being, is inscrutable and unsearchable. We do not approach God with the powers of logic, and should we try, we're sure to stumble over the rock that is the crucified Christ. Mystery is inherent to the nature of the gospel, whose wisdom confounds more than assists. God's project of salvation, in sending a suffering Servant to wash the feet of the world in his very blood, is foolishness to the world. Even faith—biblical faith—leaves us with a great deal of partial understanding. As the apostle Paul has written, faith is like seeing through a glass darkly. Just because we walk by faith doesn't mean the room is always flooded with light.

It was the fiery spectacle of paradox that halted Moses as he trailed the goats up the mountain of God. "Behold, the bush was burning, yet it was not consumed." Here, on the most ordinary of days, Moses discovered a mystery flaming up: a bush alight and yet alive. *Behold.* The biblical word *behold* is vernacular for "Stop! Pay attention! Pause! Consider!" I think about how a twenty-first-century Moses might have hurried past, how he might have proven disinterested, distracted, crossing the street to pull a buzzing phone from his pocket. I think of how the story would have gone differently had Moses failed wonder, had he resisted the compulsion, inner and quiet, to draw closer. But he didn't. And for the first time, as he neared paradox, he heard the voice of God calling his name. "Moses, Moses!" The divine encounter was a thrill—and then he was perilously warned against coming too close. "The place on which you are standing is holy ground." Life-changing encounters with God can begin with something as unremarkable as this: the unheroic decision to turn aside and pay paradox a little bit of attention.

> There's a whole lot of promise in a little bit of wondering.

When a bush is alight and yet alive, that's the very place for removing our shoes. There's a whole lot of promise in a little bit of wondering.

▲ ● ■

It was, paradoxically, the tangles of Christian faith that provided its strongest apologetic to G. K. Chesterton, late nineteenth- and early twentieth-century British writer and thinker. In his book *Orthodoxy*, Chesterton explains that Christianity's ability to maintain paradox provided convincing proof of its reliability. Chesterton believed not in spite of mystery—but because of it.

Chesterton recalled the contradictory arguments he often heard leveled against Christianity. It wasn't, for example, that Christianity was always charged with being too pessimistic; it was also criticized for being too hopeful. Some people faulted Christianity for being too meek; others faulted it for being too bold. "No sooner had my indignation died down at its angular and aggressive squareness than I was called up again to notice and condemn its enervating [debilitating] and sensual roundness."[8] If Christianity was consistently attacked, Chesterton noticed curiously that it was always attacked for inconsistent reasons. This was cause for his own little bit of wondering.

It might have been, reasoned Chesterton, that critics faulted Christianity in the same way that a short man finds another man too tall or a tall man finds another man too short. In that case, it would have been easiest to defend Christian faith as a kind of compromise, "sensible and [standing] in the middle."⁹ But as far as Chesterton could see, Christianity did not always moderate contradictions. Often, it maintained them. It affirmed the utter depravity of human beings and hope in their redemption at the same time. It preached death and resurrection in the same breath. With this and many other examples, Christianity was not to be deemed the man of average height: it was the paradox of the short man and the tall man standing upright in the same body.

As Chesterton began to discover, the emotionally satisfying part of Christianity wasn't just its linear logic; it was also its hospitality to paradox—that its facts were often its mysteries. That in both doctrine and ethic, Christianity had the capacity for affirming contradiction. According to Chesterton, we're not made to be the kind of people always painting a black and white world in dreary shades of gray—or, as Chesterton more precisely put it, a red and white world painted in ruined hues of pink. We want a saturated world of paradox, which is to say we want "the thrilling romance of Orthodoxy." A credible witness, then, is not only one that tidies drawers; it's also content to, at times, leave the drawers mussed up.

This too is paradoxical: that while as believers, we feel obliged to comb through tangles, both for ourselves and for the doubters we love, we also cherish the rich complexity of our faith and its frequent refusal to be bargained into aphorism and geometric proof.

It is paradoxical that on the one hand, listicles will sell books—and that on the other, we will yet long for truths that can't be squeezed onto billboards.

It's a mystery that we can be the kind of people insistent on seeing—and a people contented with a good degree of dark.

The psalmist described best our peacemaking with paradox when he compared us to children weaned of the appetite for answers:

> I do not occupy myself with things
>   too great and too marvelous for me.
> But I have calmed and quieted my soul,
>   like a weaned child with its mother,
>   like a weaned child is my soul within me.

There is strange rest we find in the bosom of God, even in the arms of paradox.

There might have been any number of ways I could have examined paradox for the purposes of this book. I took the only route that made sense: I examined the Scriptures. In the following pages, I have paused in four places where Scripture has given me pause:[10] at the incarnation, at the kingdom of God, at grace, and at lament. Each of these themes in Scripture is a rock to be turned over, a bush to be examined. They require us to abandon the polarities of *either* and *or* and embrace instead the dissonance of *and*. They lend themselves to certainty—and also to curiosity. They are foundational to our creeds—and yet fundamental mysteries.

The incarnation, for example, begs us to ask questions like, How can a spiritual life be so bodily? And how can dastardly human beings be meant for such glory? The kingdom inspires niggling curiosities like, How can God's work of redemption be as virulent and vulnerable as a seed? How can kingdom people, eyes fixed on eternity, also lead such worldly lives? Grace, as another example of paradox, forces us to confront the perplexing nature of God, that he is both severe and loving; the gospel cannot be reduced to saccharine sentiments. And finally, lament teaches us the paradoxical way of grieving hope. How is it that beating our fists against the chest of God can be an act of great faith? I've been caught wondering. I hope you will too.

I haven't systematically treated any of these themes, which is to say that I have not subjected them to the modern exegetical trauma described by Mike Cosper, whereby we make the Bible "a subject to be mastered, a corpse to be dissected [and] placed on a steel table and subjected to a thousand acts of violence . . . split into its component parts, footnoted for historicity and commented on from every angle."[11] As I've walked through the (sometimes dark) woods of God's Word, I haven't played the role of expert botanist but that of amateur hiker. I've wandered. I've let myself stumble over complexities. I've followed the footpaths of my own questions. When I've bent down for a closer look, it's been to puzzle over the unobvious, the seemingly contradictory, the mysterious, even the inflammatory. In other words, I haven't cataloged the entire forest, but I've noticed a few of its spectacular species.

Initially, at least, it seemed I had turned up these four themes—incarnation, kingdom, grace, and lament—like rabbits out of a hat. They were curiosities to me, although they didn't suggest a coherent interest. Only later did I realize that these four themes weren't haphazard choices but a way in which to trace the entire story of the gospel: from the birth of Jesus (the incarnation) to his public ministry (the announcement of the kingdom) to his crucifixion (the expression of divine grace), and finally, to his resurrection and ascent (the hope of humanity's lament). In all of this wondering, I've discovered how the gospel is a four-act surprise. It's a mystery, not just in its parts, but also in its whole.

This is the argument of the apostle Paul, of course, who calls out the scandals of the gospel's mystery in his many letters: "I do not want you to be unaware of this *mystery* . . . a partial hardening [that] has come upon Israel, until the fullness of the Gentiles has come in" (Rom 11:25); "Behold! I tell you a *mystery.* We shall not all sleep, but we shall all be changed" (1 Cor 15:51); "This *mystery* is that the Gentiles are fellow heirs, members of the same body, and partakers of the promise in Christ Jesus through the gospel" (Eph 3:6); "This *mystery* is profound, and I am saying that it refers to Christ and the church" (Eph 5:32); "To them God chose to make known how great among the Gentiles are the riches of the glory of this *mystery,* which is Christ in you, the hope of glory" (Col 1:27); "Great indeed, we confess, is the *mystery* of godliness: [Christ] was manifested in the flesh, vindicated by the Spirit, seen by angels, proclaimed among the nations, believed on in the world, taken up in glory" (1 Tim 3:16). The gospel, as enfleshed mystery, has strong enough arms to hold slippery things, fitful things. The story of God itself won't be buckled down and made to sit still.

This is a book about faith in its lived-in condition—as it abides complexity rather than resists it. It warns against fear and hurry, bidding us to quietly, humbly attend to the rustling leaves of divine movement, just as Moses attended to the burning bush and Samuel attended to the voice of God: "Speak, for your servant hears."

When we're surprised by paradox, we might keep still just long enough to know that he is God.

PART ONE

INCARNATION

God clothed himself with flesh and wriggled his way into the world through a womb. A new Adam came to set the record straight. Bellowing as he drank in the cold air with his lungs, this baby straightened to stretch, then drew his bony knees to his tiny ribbed chest; God was covered in the waxy vernix of humanity. The *I AM* became the *I AND*, and we have seen his glory.

It is a paradox that the glorious God who spoke the world into being chose to make himself this small—and a paradox that he could be so ambitious for the glory of the creatures he came to save.

1

THE GREAT I AND

*T*his book began in a counselor's office.

I don't like admitting that something was going wrong in my life. But something was going wrong, and I had no immediate solution, if such a word can be applied to the travail of being human.

For years, I had been hurtling myself at a family member's heavyweight bag of sorrows. I was bruised, and the bag was not giving. There was a growing feeling of powerlessness, burdensome in its own right, but there was also the clear recognition that, even as I tried helping, I was being lied to. On a routine basis. The lies were sometimes so petty as to be ridiculous—deceptions of setting, not plot. At other times, the lies were consequential and hurtful. It was becoming more and more difficult to know which words weren't stolen, which scenes weren't edited, which narratives weren't fictionalized. I knew very little of the truth, but at least I knew this much: I could only help if I had the facts.

For years, this blood relationship suspended me in emotional indecision. I had given the advice, made the phone calls, shelled out the cash, paid the visits, prayed and prayed harder, but there was no staunching the bleeding. On the one hand, I hesitated to attribute moral guilt to what might have been a real case of pathology. This was a person who had suffered the trauma of other people's bad decisions—suffered it long, suffered it young. If this person was a victim, wasn't it my greatest kindness to choose silence as a way of choosing love? But on the other hand, I grew less and less willing to be played for a fool, less and less certain that feigned ignorance was even helping. There was no easy deciding who was victim and perpetrator; there was no easy concluding that I would, in fact, be the hero of this story.

For months, I played court stenographer as one way of keeping straight the twist of the stories. Whenever we'd speak by phone, I'd record what was said as one reliable way to prove that I wasn't the one losing my mind. But once the record had accumulated and I finally confronted the inconsistencies, warning that I would call whoever necessary to confirm the story, the threat was met with bravado: *sure, go ahead, you'll see that I'm telling the truth.* I hated my suspicion, hated its necessity, hated most that if I made the call, the relationship was sure to fall in shards at my feet.

I did call. And there was broken glass. Then came silence, long and protracted, the forceful, deliberate cutting off. I was torn out of this person's life like pictures of a high school girlfriend from the yearbook. And this fracture is what I came to report to the counselor on a sunny June day as the noise machine whirred in the hallway. I needed to know if she thought me cruel for choosing the confrontation. I needed greater understanding of the suffering of mental illness. Most importantly, I needed light for groping my way out of this tunnel with two exits: should I suffer the lying or sever the relationship?

"What if there's a third way?" she asked gently. Her question sounded like a struck bell, especially because "third way" language was something my spiritual director often used with me. It was as if here was yet another invitation to find a sure-footed way on some undiscovered path—to find *and* where I had previously imagined only *either* and *or*. Here was an invitation to "lean not on my own understanding" and find wisdom in the way of paradox.

I went to a counselor looking for tidy answers about a broken relationship. I wanted those answers, as I often do, to rid me of the anguish of self-doubt. It's the easing of guilt that often fuels my desire for a more black-and-white world. What I found instead on that sunny summer day was a proposition requiring greater patience and prayer: that God, infinitely creative in his own nature, **The paradox of the incarnation reminds us that God is the author of *both* and *and*.** was suggesting infinitely more creative possibilities than I had previously considered. I began to learn then that it is God who walks through the walls we frame around an idea or problem, God who breaks the bonds of our *eithers* and *ors*. I began to understand that when I asked for one-word answers from God, when I wanted faith to read like instructions from Ikea, I was likely asking the wrong kinds of questions.

As the first part of this book suggests, it's the paradox of the incarnation that reminds us that God is the author of *both* and *and*.

▲ ● ■

John Murray has written that orthodoxy plays the role of conjunction: not *either*, not *or*, but *and*. "The thought of incarnation is stupendous, for it means the conjunction in one person of all that belongs to godhead and all that belongs to manhood."[1] To clothe himself with flesh, God himself has practiced what seems to be an eternal contradiction called love. In Jesus, God did not set aside his godhood to assume the liabilities of human flesh. He did not, as it were, turn in his "God" badge at the door of the Milky Way. Instead, the *I* AM assumed humanity as a second nature while remaining fully God. God *and* man, man *and* God. "This mystery cannot be comprehended," writes Herman Bavinck. "It can only be gratefully acknowledged." Bavinck helpfully adds, "Mystery and self-contradiction are not synonymous."[2] In other words, just because it can't be explained doesn't make it false.

As the apostle Paul acknowledged frequently in his writings, the greatest mystery of Christian faith is the incarnation. "Great indeed," writes Paul, citing an early Christian hymn, "is the mystery of godliness:

> He was manifested in the flesh,
>> vindicated by the Spirit,
>> seen by angels,
> proclaimed among the nations,
>> believed on in the world,
>>> taken up in glory. (1 Tim 3:16)

The incarnation is God's burning bush: a mystery demanding a closer look.

The word *mystery* appears twenty-eight times in the New Testament and only a handful of times in one Old Testament book, the book of Daniel (2:18-19, 27-30, 47; 4:6). In Daniel, as well as in the later apostolic writings, mystery refers to the hidden things soon to be revealed by God. They aren't uncertainties insomuch as, according to Vine's, they are "outside the range of unassisted natural apprehension [and] can be made known only by divine revelation, and [are] made known in a manner and time appointed by God, and to those only who are illumined by His Spirit."[3] What was dark and hidden in the Old Testament, although not entirely absent, was the expectation that God would condescend to become human, clothing himself with flesh. The *I* AM would become the *I* AND.

The incarnation is not the familiar idea in Greek and Roman mythologies of gods disguising themselves temporarily as humans to visit humanity; nor is it the idea of gods mating with mortal women to produce demi-gods. God did not sleep with the virgin Mary to produce a superhuman, and God did not play the part of Jesus of Nazareth until the curtain drew at the hour of his crucifixion and he shed his fleshly disguise. As the New Testament writers clearly asserted, Jesus was fully god and fully human, and after his scandalous execution, he was bodily resurrected, his scarred palms and pierced side still bearing the evidence of his cruel torture. When Mary Magdalene met the resurrected Jesus outside his tomb, she hadn't expected it would be him and mistook him for the gardener. When she finally learned his identity, she clung to him. Even now, seated in heaven, Jesus remains God-and-man: advocating for his brothers and sisters whose weakness and frailty he bodily knows.

On the day when faith is made sight and we find ourselves face-to-face with Jesus, he will still be the Great I AND.

Psalm 19 illuminates the methods of this self-revealing God of love: that first he reveals himself through creation. In even the most remote corners of the earth, the sky speaks of God. God allows his glory to be seen in the blinking, dotted night sky, in the burnished colors of dusk, in the creeping radiance of dawn. But we might say that creation plays clear but indistinct notes of God's eternal power and divine nature, which is why Psalm 19 moves to a less ambiguous method of God's self-revelation: the perfection, wisdom, rightness, and surety of God's precepts, commandments, and rules. As the law itself reminds us, the speaking, self-revealing God spoke to his people from Sinai, handing down the abundant ways by which they were to follow him and live. "By them is your servant warned; in keeping them there is great reward." God's Word speaks for and about him, and his law is an expression of his love.

But Psalm 19 does not stop with the speech of the skies or with the witness of the law of the Lord. As if from the back of the room, we hear the voice of man himself, clamoring to speak of God: "Let the words of my mouth and the meditation of my heart be acceptable in your sight, O LORD, my rock and my redeemer." He is a fallible creature and recognizes his proclivity for hidden fault and presumptuous sin. I do not speak as well as creation, he seems to confess. I cannot match the perfection of the law, he concedes. And yet he prays: *Let me be a witness too.*

Imagine, then, that the psalmist's prayer is answered most decisively when God clothes himself with flesh and wriggles his way into the world through a womb—a new Adam coming to set the record straight. He is the Word made flesh. Bellowing as he drinks in the cold air with his lungs, this baby straightens to stretch, then draws his bony knees to his tiny ribbed chest; God is covered in the waxy vernix of humanity. No longer satisfied with the partial revelation of himself, bent on driving away the blinding rain that darkens hearts, God clamors for greater fullness, for clearer visibility than creation and the law and sinful humanity could ever offer. Because God so loved the world, he gave his Son to show his face.

The incarnation—the paradox of God made human—teaches us to look for God in the *and*.

▲ ● ■

"You and Ryan seemed tired Friday," Janey said when she saw me at church. "Everything okay?" We had been to their house for a Christmas party two days earlier.

"Oh, we weren't tired," I said, laughing. "We were fighting." The sky had been falling in thick flakes that Friday, the city roads becoming a congested crawl under a whitened sky. A few more stolen moments in the car alone had afforded just enough time for an argument.

> The incarnation— the paradox of God made human— teaches us to look for God in the *and*.

"When are you taking your vacation days?" I had asked Ryan days earlier. It wasn't exactly his answer that I had been brooding about for days and finally took up on the way to Janey's. He did, in fact, plan to catch up while the office was quiet over the Christmas holidays. Instead, it was more that he hadn't asked me the same question, carelessly presuming that I either had no pressing deadlines or that I would squirrel away time for meeting them as I had made a convenient habit of doing. This has been a recurrent place of tension in the middle years of our marriage, this sharing of domestic responsibility, this supporting of other respective ambitions.

I don't relish an argument, but neither have I wanted the kind of polite and distant marriage my own parents modeled for me. After twenty odd years at this domestic project, I've come to believe that it isn't the absence of conflict that makes for a happy, stable marriage. Our wedding vows don't simply bind us to the politeness of *yes*; they also bind us to the courage of *and*, which is to say the bravery of moving toward places of paradox. In Christian marriage, we choose to love, serve, and submit to one another, even on the days that wring us out bone-tired. But Christian marriage isn't built on mute self-sacrifice alone. We must also learn to practice rigorous, risky honesty. We name our desires (however fearfully) and admit our disappointments (however angrily). Yes is the daily work of marital faithfulness; and is our practiced resistance to apathy. In marriage, I am, paradoxically, called to a daily dying and a daily showing up—because as the Holy Spirit has whispered, "There is only one wife in this relationship." It is a lot of muddled, messy work, especially when you try doing it on the way to a dinner party.

Marriage demands that we abide paradox, that we hold to principles at variance with one another, not in spite of love but because of it. And we know from Scripture that marital love is a picture of God's love for his church (cf. Eph 5). God said yes and and in Christ to love the world well. The incarnation is the act of God fulfilling all his promises with his own hearty yes of Christ (cf. 2 Cor 1:20). In the incarnation, God embraced contradiction in his own being and sustained tension in his own flesh. The incarnation suggests to God's people the holy possibilities of and, this little word that rests at the bottom of every paradox. It reminds us that God's ways will surprise us more than we think.

There is virtue in the little word and, a humility that it can form in us. And helped the early church learn to love each other well. It wasn't easy when the contradictions of Jew and Gentile were joined together in the holy matrimony of Christ's body; God was reconciling tremendous difference for the sake of unity in his new kingdom of priests. How were these people to eat dinner together, much less share a common faith? There were very practical questions to resolve when the Gentiles were grafted into the people of God: did they need to be circumcised and keep kosher? When Peter stood in the assembly of God's people, he was clear to commend grace, not law-keeping, as the basis for salvation: "We believe that we will be saved through the grace of the Lord Jesus."

But grace didn't settle the matter entirely. The church kept insisting on *and*: exercise your freedom *and* love your brother. Obey your own conscience *and* "pursue what makes for peace and for mutual upbuilding." There was liberty in Christ to eat freely and gratefully, *and* there was also the constraining obligation to love. "If your brother is grieved by what you eat, you are no longer walking in love" (Rom 14:15). This little three-letter word *and* had the power to bind together a church that might easily have been polarized by their food preferences and their festal calendars. As the apostle Paul outlines in Romans 14, care needed to be exercised for belonging as well as for belief. In fact, Paul deliberately withholds arbitrating some of the debates of his day (Do we eat meat or merely vegetables? Do we observe the Sabbath or esteem every day alike?) and insists instead on this: that our brothers and sisters are worthy of honor, and that each of us will stand before the judgment seat of God.

"Do not, for the sake of food, destroy the work of God."

Imagine *and* as a measure of healing some of the hostilities of our either-or world. Indeed, that's something suggested by moral psychologist Jonathan Haidt in his book *The Righteous Mind*. As his subtitle illustrates, Haidt seeks to understand "why good people are divided by politics and religion." He posits a moral foundations theory, which teases out five different emphases in human morality: care (vs. harm), fairness (vs. cheating), loyalty (vs. betrayal), authority (vs. subversion), and sanctity (vs. degradation). A major difference between political liberals and political conservatives, Haidt writes, is the relative degree of importance they'd ascribe to each of these areas. As his research has shown, liberals are most concerned with care and fairness while conservatives tend to grant equal importance to all five. It's not simply that liberals or conservatives are more or less concerned with morality, rather their conceptions of morality differ in concern. Haidt believes there's a mutual respect to be built according to his research: that our society will flourish from the counterbalance of varying perspectives. We're helped beyond polarization and paralysis, in his words, by an "and" approach.

In this book, I'm inviting readers to imagine the possibilities of *and.* I am not, however, dismissing that *either* and *or* are God's words too. As philosopher Isaiah Berlin has written, "I am not a relativist. I do not say 'I like my coffee with milk and you like it without. I am in favor of kindness and you prefer concentration camps.'"[4] Scripture's revelation is often less murky than we wish, especially for deciding many contemporary ethical issues at the center of fierce public debate. However much to our chagrin, God is not afraid to pronounce, "Thou shalt" and "Thou shalt not."

Yet one important lesson of paradox is that we are not always confined to choosing between two dreaded alternatives. Faith doesn't always divide the world into two clean halves of right and wrong. In those places of seeming paralysis, such as I describe at the opening of this chapter, when *either* and *or* seem to bind our hands, we can surrender our straightjacketed imagination and look for the creativity of the incarnate God—And the love of the great *I* AND.

2

ANNUNCIATIONS

*A*t the end of November, Mary Szybist's book of poetry, *Incarnadine*, landed like the angel Gabriel on the front stoop, just in time for Advent. Szybist's poems recast Mary's surprise news of unplanned pregnancy in unexpected places: cornfields and birthday parties, in the rose garden and at the kitchen sink. "I think I see annunciations everywhere!"[1] As Advent began, I read Szybist's poetry to shadow the mystery of God become man, to catch a glimpse of him. "Tell me you believe the world is made of more than all its stupid, stubborn, small refusals, that anything, everything is still possible."[2]

In those first few days of Advent, I was not only reading Szybist's poetry, I was also playing on repeat Morten Lauridsen's choral work *O Magnum Mysterium*: "O great mystery and wondrous sacrament, that animals should see their newborn Lord lying in a manger!" The melodies, quivering and hushed, full and jubilant, bear witness to the still and holy point of the turning world—that moment when God burst from a womb. I played it in the kitchen and imagined the whole world filling with *Alleluia*.

Advent was briefly consecrated. Then December awoke in distemper. I had planned for contemplative stillness; I had instead end-of-year financial accounting and tense marital conversations about money. I had hoped for quiet; I prepared instead to host out-of-town family for the holidays. Twenty people were coming for Christmas Eve dinner. Did I have enough silverware? Enough twine to truss the chickens? The immigration lawyer called with the good news that we had passed into the second stage of our Canadian permanent residency application, the bad news that we needed to complete a ten-year travel and address history, schedule a medical exam for all seven of us, and get more photos taken before the start of the new year. Advent was not taming the beast of daily life.

When Morten Lauridsen received, in 1993, the commission to write the choral composition for *O Magnum Mysterium*, he took inspiration from a painting by early baroque Spanish master Francisco de Zurbarán. Drawn into the dark atmospheric canvas of Zurbarán's *Still Life with Lemons, Oranges and a Rose* (1633), Lauridsen describes his reaction: "Before it one tends to speak in hushed tones, if at all."

The canvas portrays a precisely arranged row of three objects: a silver plate of citrons (Spanish cousin to the lemon); a woven basket of oranges, freshly plucked with leaves and blossoms; another silver plate with a two-handled ceramic cup of water and a rose blossom. Because Zurbarán made his living on religious commissions, art critics argue that the three objects represent sacrificial offerings to the Virgin Mary. Peter Schjeldahl of the *New Yorker* says the piece "invests ordinary comestibles on a piece of domestic furniture with the gravitas of a sacrificial altar." In other words, the canvas turns something household into something holy. And this is precisely what Lauridsen meant to capture in his choral work: the small, ordinary wonder of a stable scene, where animals were first witnesses to the crowning of the newborn King.

Zurbarán's canvas does not stoke the religious imagination with a majestic sweep of the sky or an expansive stretch of mountains but with today's picks from the garden and a small cup of water. The table made altar invites the viewer to worship. In color and line and composition, Zurbarán's work indulges no avarice for the monumental. "I think I see annunciations everywhere," Zurbarán seemed to say. Even at the table.

As Zurbarán and Lauridsen seemed to understand, the incarnation is the paradox of finding God not just in the cloister but in the bodily and material conditions of the everyday. The spiritual life is meant for Sunday—*and* for the other six days too.

I know this—and I forget this. Like my daughter, who complains to me one night that life is too cluttered with the banal and that God gets crowded out by the mundane, I also get tricked into thinking that the world must quiet around me if I mean to meet God. I forget the paradox of the burning bush: that Moses met God at Horeb on an unspectacular day, that his encounter with God was less planned and more happenstance. God did not speak to Moses as the prophet sat cross-legged and silent, his hands folded in reverent prayer. God blazed up in the landscape of an ordinary Wednesday afternoon. And this seems to be how it goes with God: a spiritual life is a material one.

Despite all my spiritual intentions, Advent plunked me down, not in reverie but in the housekeeping. It had me washing lettuce—*and* thinking of Zechariah's surprise at seeing the angel Gabriel

during an ordinary shift at the temple. It had me chopping carrots—
and thinking of Joseph, waking to tangled sheets, disturbed by a
dream. My eyes burning from the onions, Advent had me thinking
of Mary, mother of God, taking into her leaking breasts all the
blinding mysteries of the Son of God's birth, her heart so full of
wondering. I'm sure that they, like me, never expected to find God
in such ordinary places. But that's one of the surprises of the incarnation: that God should stoop to dignify our skin and this little
patch of land called earth.

It's a paradox that the spiritual life, for all its presumed holiness,
can be so distinctly unspiritual.

▲ ● ■

I don't want to suggest that the biblical story can be simplisti-
cally reduced into one sentence. Or maybe I do. *Follow the food.*

> **It's a paradox that the spiritual life, for all its presumed holiness, can be so distinctly unspiritual.**

In Genesis 1, we meet a God insistent
on feeding his hungry people. "Behold, I
have given you every plant yielding seed
that is on the face of all the earth, and every
tree with seed in its fruit. You shall have
them for food." If humanity's pressing
question seems always to be, "What shall we eat?" God took the
liberty of answering it at the very beginning of time. Stretching his
arm over the bounty of creation, he indicated every peach tree, every
honeysuckle vine, every potato root, every banana tree. Take and
eat: it's my gift of grace. God's people were fed by his hand, made
guests at his table. Earth was a heavenly place.

The fall from that state of grace was, of course, a matter of food.
In Genesis 2, God indicates that he has given every tree from the

Garden as food for his people; one tree, however, has been forbidden. "You shall not eat of the fruit of the tree that is in the midst of the garden, neither shall you touch it, lest you die" (Gen 3:3). The serpent cunningly suggested to Eve that there were good reasons for eating this tree, namely, that one could have the infinite, infallible wisdom of God. Suckered, Eve took a second look. When she did, however, divine wisdom wasn't the only reason for eating the forbidden fruit. "The woman saw that the tree was good *for food*" (v. 6). Humanity's first sin was as bodily as it was spiritual; idolatry was also a matter of appetite.

We follow the food out of the book of Genesis and meet an exiled Moses, standing before a bush that burns but is not consumed. The God of Abraham appears to him in the wilderness of Sinai to announce a promise: "I have come down to deliver [my people] out of the hand of the Egyptians and to bring them up out of that land to a good and broad land, a land flowing with *milk and honey*" (Ex 3:8). God's goodness is not the dry crust of abstraction. It has taste and smell, just as it did in the Garden—even if later, after their deliverance, the Israelites pine for the menu of slavery. "We remember the fish we ate in Egypt that cost nothing, the cucumbers, the melons, the leeks, the onions, and the garlic" (Num 11:5). In the story of Israel, food seems always to be the thing that leads to and away from God.

In fact, it's food that damns the people of Israel in the proclamations of the prophets. Hosea announces that Israel has followed the food straight into the arms of other gods.

> She said, "I will go after my lovers,
>   who give me my bread and my water,
>   my wool and my flax, my oil and my drink." (Hos 2:5)

God says,

> She did not know
>   that it was I who gave her
>   the grain, the wine, and the oil. (v. 8)

God's generous table-laying had not been received with thanks-giving. Instead, his goodness was credited to idols. And as if finally fed up with their idolatrous betrayal of his gifts, God takes these gifts of the table away. The people are exiled, the fields left fallow. Joel cries out,

> The fields are destroyed,
>   the ground mourns,
> because the grain is destroyed,
>   the wine dries up,
>   the oil languishes. (Joel 1:10)

The food disappears, and with it God—or so it seems to his people. This makes Habakkuk's faith even more remarkable:

> Though the fig tree should not blossom,
>   nor fruit be on the vines,
> the produce of the olive fail
>   and the fields yield no food,
> the flock be cut off from the fold
>   and there be no herd in the stalls,
> yet I will rejoice in the Lord;
>   I will take joy in the God of my salvation. (Hab 3:17-18)

Food or no food, Habakkuk will worship.

Turning the pages to the New Testament, we are quickly ushered into the presence of Jesus. His first "test" is refusing the food of the devil, who tempts him to turn stones into bread. The incarnate God, himself a hungry man, is followed by hungry crowds throughout the pages of the Gospels. On one such day, the sermon spent, the sun setting, the God-man gives instructions for thousands to sit for the meal. He takes the small lunch of a little boy. He blesses it. He multiplies it into feast. His disciples distribute the miracle, and twelve baskets full of God's leftovers are collected when the people have had their fill. It is a lesson for the stomach *and* the spirit: God is he who feeds.

On the following day, when Jesus exegetes his miracle, he tells them the meaning behind the loaves. "I am the bread of life," Jesus said. "Whoever comes to me shall not hunger, and whoever believes in me shall never thirst" (Jn 6:35). As if stretching his arm over the bounty of creation, he indicates his own body. Take and eat; it is a gift of grace. At the incarnation of God, God himself became food for us, and it's his story that we remember in a meal. Our future with him is promised as feast.

Follow the food is one way of saying that the incarnation is a kind of hermeneutic of God's story. It teaches us to embrace the material world rather than despise it. To understand something about God, about the life of faith, we will need something more than contemplative souls, something more than cerebral agility, something more than big theological words. We will need bodies. We will need lettuce leaves. We will need leaky breasts and someone to tell us to *taste* and see that the Lord is good.

We are tempted to look for God in the invisible, in the intangible, in the ethereal—and the God of Spirit is invisible, intangible, and ethereal. But the incarnation is also the death of abstraction. Salvation came through a body, redemption through a man. An unbounded, incorporeal God of Spirit clothed himself with flesh and entered the world of matter, never fearing that the act would sully his holiness.

> We must realize that the Christian message does not at its heart express a concept or an idea. . . . All the [theological] concepts and ideas . . . (God, man, world, eternity, time, even salvation, grace, transgression, atonement, and any others) can derive their significance only from the bearer of this name and from His history, and not the reverse. . . . They can only serve to describe this name—the name of Jesus Christ.[3]

I might say it like this: our story about God reads like a good poem. A good poem doesn't parlay hollow, abstract phrases—even if they rhyme. It enfleshes. It traffics in the concrete. To be sure, there are multisyllabic parts to life with God, and theology has a vocabulary for explaining those parts. But even the big words are derived from a story of bread and wine, blood and water, parting seas, torn veils, bodies made temples, the very good stuff of a very good world created and redeemed by a very good God-man. I wonder if this is the way that we, post-Enlightenment, tend to tell it.

Part of the brilliance of Tish Harrison Warren's award-winning *Liturgy of the Ordinary* is the invitation to see God in the most banal moments of the everyday: as we wake up in the morning with rumpled hair; as we stand in front of the mirror, brushing our teeth; as we stare at the computer screen, checking our email. An open-faced peanut butter and jelly sandwich on the cover, the book takes us by the face and turns our head in the direction of seeing God—not in the sky, as the apostles tried searching for Jesus after his ascent, but on earth. "Men of Galilee, why do you stand looking into heaven?"

During Advent, I had looked for God in the cloister. I should have known to look for him in the kitchen.

▲ ● ■

It is a paradox that we find God at church—and find him in conversation with a stranger on the subway. It is a paradox that we keep still to know that God is God—and that our lives, with all their sacred responsibilities, can hustle us as much as they do. It is a paradox that the freckles on my child's nose can, like contemplation of the cross, be such sudden cause for worship. The temple was filled with the fragrance of God—and his bushes burned in the wide expanse of the world.

Orthodox theologian Alexander Schmemann reminds us, in his book *For the Life of the World*, that humanity's story begins and ends at God's banqueting table. In the Garden, there was no artificial division of life into the spiritual and the material, the sacred and the profane, the supernatural and the natural. Everything that existed was "God's gift to man, and it all exist[ed] to make God known to man, to make man's life communion with God."[4] There was no needed suspicion of the body or of creation.

Sin, according to Schmemann, was not simply that man loved the material; it was that he *loved it for itself*. Sin severed the material from the spiritual—the food from God. "Man ate the forbidden fruit. The fruit of that one tree, whatever else it might signify, was unlike every other fruit in the Garden: it was not offered as a gift to man. Not given, not blessed by God, it was food whose eating was condemned to be communion with itself alone, and not with God. It is the image of the world loved for itself, and eating it is the image of life understood as an end of itself."[5]

The first sin was not only our love of the gift, it was our preference for the gift over the Giver. Sin distorted our relationship to the material world. Creation was no longer a means of knowing and serving and praising God, but a means of satisfying our own greedy appetites. And because of that first sin, our bodies were no longer a source of freedom and unabashed pleasure, but a source of fear and shame.

A return to God is not a detachment from our bodies and the material world. The holiest people live the crustiest lives. They garden and have sex, pay bills and vacuum. Early church father Origen purportedly castrated himself in a fit of religious ecstasy, violently cutting off his "right hand" as Jesus had commanded might sometimes be necessary. Perhaps Origen needed to live without his sex. Or perhaps, as the Second Council of Constantinople agreed in 553, Origen was a heretic for, among other things, his rejection of the goodness of the material world. Like Origen or like the Colossians before him, our great heresy might not only be our godless hedonism but our godless asceticism (cf. Col 2:16-23). Is it too much to say, with Talmudic tradition, that we might be judged not just for stolen pleasures but for every rightful pleasure we've chosen to forfeit? Judged for our insistence on a purely spiritual life?

Surely the incarnation is a bid into God's gloriously real world of "rocks and trees, of skies and seas." Surely, as C. S. Lewis illustrates in *The Great Divorce*, hell is the most spiritual of places, heaven the most real. Of course, our love of the material must be a rightly ordered love—a subordinate love which recognizes that we are hungry for God and that "all desire is finally a desire for Him."[6] As the psalmist knew clearly, nothing in all of creation apart from him can satisfy the hungry human heart. There is nothing to buy, nothing to strive to own that can fill our need of God.

One predicament of faith is that it can be so unabashedly material. It sees the condescension of God everywhere. Schmemann would say that we rightly order our relationship to the material world when we return to humanity's original vocation: Eucharist. We receive all that God has given with joy and gratitude, and then we offer it—along with ourselves—back to God.

When my high school-age daughter asks me, leaning against her bedroom door as we talk late one night, how she can make room for God when her calendar bulges with activities and end-of-the-year assignments, I remind her of this paradox: annunciations aren't just the angelic surprises of monasteries and quiet mornings. They land on the front stoop, at the kitchen sink, in the office, in band rehearsal. God has set the world alight with his presence. We just need eyes to see . . .

> One predicament of faith is that it can be so unabashedly material.

And mouths opened wide for filling.

3

ONE WILD AND
PRECIOUS LIFE

*W*hen we moved to Toronto in 2011, because several days were needed to inventory the contents of our moving truck at the Canadian border, our family spent a long weekend visiting Niagara Falls. It was the first family "vacation" we'd taken since the arrival of our twin boys, then three and a half, Costco having been our biggest adventure until that point. Gratefully, at the Falls no one tumbled overboard on our Maid of the Mist tour, and we managed to snap a picture of Colin, cloaked in a yellow plastic poncho, walking with his hands folded—a little monk on his way to prayer.

In the earliest years of having five young children, the days blurred one into another. It was a strict cycle of rinse and repeat: nurse the babies, feed the other three, make sure we all have enough clean underwear. I had tried starting a blog during those years—and gave it up after the third post in which I'd mixed up modifiers, confusing whether I had wiped the bottom of my child or my husband. But after we moved to Toronto, and especially after Colin and Andrew started preschool, a few mornings afforded some quiet, and I started to write again in the bright, sunny porch office at the front of the house. A dam released; the words came in torrents.

"I think God's asking me to start a blog," I told Ryan on a fall afternoon as we walked, the kids racing ahead of us in our neighborhood ravine. I was sheepish to admit the idea, and we both easily dismissed it. There was something grossly self-preoccupied about blogs, we both thought. The world did not need one more blogger calling out her specialness to the world.

Yet the idea persisted.

It persisted not least because I had recently finished writing thirty days of devotional copy on the topic of the fear of the Lord. As I studied to write, I realized how much of Israel's sin was bound up in the fear that resulted from spiritual forgetfulness. Psalm 78 speaks to this malady of spiritual amnesia, opening with a commendation to pass down stories from generation to generation "so that [the children] should set their hope in God and not forget the works of God, but keep his commandments." To forget was to tempt the fate of stubbornness, a sin into which previous generations of Israelites had fallen. To fail memory was to insure hearts that were not steadfast and spirits that were not faithful to God.

In their forty years of wilderness wandering, the Israelites lived the rebellion of chronic forgetting: "They forgot his works and the wonders he had shown them." God had delivered them from Egypt with irrefutable feats of glory. The plagues. The parting of the Red Sea. His people had danced on the banks on that great body of water where the bodies of Egyptian soldiers had washed up. God had led them by a pillar of cloud by day, a tower of fire by night. He'd split rocks in the wilderness to give "them drink abundantly as from the deep." And yet, when their stomachs grumbled, they doubted the power and provision of God. "Can God spread a table in the wilderness?" They failed memory, which is another way of saying they failed faith. What might have been different for Israel if they had rehearsed their story, if they'd made it their regular practice to remember all that God had done on their behalf?

Looking back might have made all the difference for moving ahead.

Israel didn't keep their story, and as a result, they didn't keep the faith. But if I've made it sound so obvious and straightforward, this imperative to keep one's story, it isn't. I once heard a moderator of a panel of Christian writers put this question to the participants: "How do you keep God's story prominent in your writing rather than your own?" I've puzzled over that question for years, understanding, on the one hand, the fear that we're raising up a generation of people who know no truth beyond their personal experience, who do not understand their stories as windows into the bigger, grander story of God. And still, I can't help wondering just how exactly to point to the place where my story ends and God's story begins. When God rained bread on his hungry people and opened rivers from rocks, whose story was that?

I think of Amanda Berry Smith, born into slavery in 1837 and called later to be God's evangelist. Having only three months of formal education, she penned her autobiography, which she titled *The Story of the Lord's Dealings with Mrs. Amanda Smith, the Colored Evangelist: Containing an Account of Her Life, Work of Faith, and Her Travels in America, England, Ireland, Scotland, India, and Africa as an Independent Missionary.*[1] In her book, Smith details an encounter with the Lord that helped her overcome fear and set her on the blazing path of missionary work around the world. "'O,' I thought, 'if there was a platform around the world I would be willing to get on it and walk and tell everybody about this sanctifying power of God!"[2] In her book, Smith told the story of her wild and precious life, a story that was never meant to leave God behind. The Lord's "dealings" with Amanda Berry Smith were, to use the language of Psalm 78, his "works" and his "wonders." Her story was hers—and her story was God's.

It's a paradox that the Lord could have dealings with Amanda Berry Smith—and a paradox that he could have dealings with me and with you. It's a paradox—a predicament, even—that my story, that your story, could be a way of proclaiming the bigger, grander story of God.

What a terrific surprise that worship can lift our eyes both upward *and* inward.

▲ ● ■

When fourth-century church father Athanasius wrote his treatise on the incarnation, he anticipated questions, not just about God entering the material world but about God's assuming the indignity of a body. "Some may then ask, why did He not manifest Himself by means of other and nobler parts of creation, and use some nobler instrument, such as sun or moon or stars or fire or air, instead of mere man?"[3]

Why would God condescend to inhabit a body that sweats and smells and betrays common courtesies in bed and at the dinner table? Wouldn't a celestial object have been more appropriately dazzling for God's house? No, Athanasius answers. God needed a body to complete the work of redemption. There was no saving us without becoming like us, no restoring the image of man without bearing it, no defeating death without dying. "He, the mighty One, the Artificer of all Himself prepared this body in the virgin as a temple for Himself, and took it for His very own."[4] Inglorious though it seemed compared to the glory of Solomon's temple, affronted as we are at the thought, a human body became God's home.

The body would seem to be a kind of predicament in the spiritual life. It's so inordinately material and messy. But the paradox of the bodily predicament for many of us is this: that the temptations of the body lie not just in the form of indulgence but also in evasion. We aren't only tempted by the gluttonous pleasures of food and sex and alcohol. No, our sins are also ones of abstraction. We can be seduced into thinking that God's story is hovering at 30,000 feet, that it's being written in the outer hemisphere of "heaven" rather than in the headlines of this earthly life. It's a paradox that we could pay too little attention to the Lord—and too little attention to the

> **The paradox of God's story is that he's chosen to write its timelessness in the ticking heart of his Son and that he's choosing to write it in our ticking hearts too.**

Lord's dealings with us. The paradox of God's story is that he's chosen to write its timelessness in the ticking heart of his Son and that he's choosing to write it in our ticking hearts too.

If I might say it like this, the incarnation, which gives us a theology of the body, tells us that God is not in the business of producing stock furniture. A bodily life, which is to say a spiritual life, is a scandalously particular life. A *special* life. The incarnation, resting as it does on the paradox of particularity, reminds us of this. Jesus was the second Adam, born of God, born of Mary. But his life is not simply a model of universality. God narrowed infinite possibilities to become a particular man in the fullness of time. Matthew and Luke open their Gospels with genealogies, which situate Jesus in a particular family line: Jesus, son of Abraham, Judah, David; Jesus, son of Rehoboam, Asaph, Uzziah; Jesus, son of Jechoniah, Azor, Eliud.

In the incarnation, God didn't absent himself from space and time; he invaded it, coming to earth at a particular moment in history: "in the days of Herod, king of Judea" (Lk 1:5). Although Jesus is, of course, a high priest in the order of Melchizedek, who "is without father or mother or genealogy, having neither beginning of days nor end of life" (Heb 7:3), he was also the son of a poor carpenter named Joseph. If there is a certain timelessness to God's story in Jesus, we might also imagine the story radically changed if he had shown up as a child laborer in Victorian England, the setting of salvation the setting of a Dickens novel. We learn to be human from Jesus, but this isn't to say that Jesus was a generic human.

A writer friend was recently asked by a pastor to share a list of resources on "biblical womanhood." She shared her bewilderment in a private Facebook group. "The Bible," someone wryly suggested.

> In the incarnation, God didn't absent himself from space and time; he invaded it, coming to earth at a particular moment in history.

Then we wondered aloud if the most pressing question for the church today was defining general, one-size-fits-all principles of biblical manhood and womanhood—or helping women and men form the discernment necessary for navigating the particularities, which is to say the "special-ness" of their lives. Was God, in other words, up to something as generic as *womanhood* and *manhood* in each of our lives—or was there more to be discovered for living our unique, embodied lives of faithfulness? Did it matter that I lived in

Toronto while my friend lived in Appalachia? That I was married to a corporate executive and she to a pastor? Did the wild and varied colors of our lives suggest wild and varied acts of obedience? Or was holiness a more monochromatic project than that?

We're sometimes left with the idea that holiness will swallow us whole, the Spirit taking up such important room in our lives that no room will be left for the selves called you, called me. But the book of Revelation portrays a different kind of perfect world. In the world beyond this one, we are not stirred into the grand melting pot of God, every distinguishing feature of our lives reduced to an ugly shade of molten muck. No, the apostle John looks at the sea of faces and sees a glorious canvas of human distinction:

> I looked, and behold, a great multitude that no one could number, from every nation, from all tribes and peoples and languages, standing before the throne and before the Lamb, clothed in white robes, with palm branches in their hands, and crying out with a loud voice, "Salvation belongs to our God who sits on the throne, and to the Lamb!" (Rev 7:9-10)

Though we sing a collective song of praise in eternity, we sing it in the particular timbre of our own voices. Though we are finally gathered as the single people of people, we are not a faceless mass of humanity. Sin, like dross, is burned away: specialness is not.

I wonder what might change for all of us to pay attention to the incarnational details of our lives: the parents to whom we were born, the places where we were raised, the losses we have suffered, the privileges we enjoy. What might it mean that I seek not simply to be the shapeless form of a biblical woman, but Jen? That you seek not simply to be something as generic as a biblical man, but John?

What unique and good work would we find to do in the world? What special praise to give to the God of particular love, who has numbered the hairs on our heads? What dignity would be gained in these sighing seventy or eighty years, which we must number with wisdom and also make glad? "Let your work be shown to your servants, and your glorious power to their children."

If only to let our wild and precious lives tell the singular story of God—here and ever after.

▲ ● ■

The human project can be grossly self-preoccupied. This is what the panel moderator understood when he asked the question, "How do you keep God's story prominent in your writing rather than your own?" Nevertheless, like Peter in John 21, for all our impious navel gazing, we can also become paradoxically entangled by our preoccupation with the lives of others. This is especially true in the age of social media, where the points of comparison multiply infinitely. On the one hand, while we crave a special life, we also want a safe life. And there is nothing safer than drawing a template to lay over our lives, scissoring with precision at the lines: Christians in the shape of gingerbread men. In that case we could exercise bullet-proof certainty that we are in the right places, doing the right things. But as Jesus scolds Peter, who asked about the future facing the beloved disciple, another man or woman's calling is not our concern: "If it is my will that he remain until I come, what is that to you? You follow me!" (Jn 21:22). *You*, follow me: you with your skin, you with your salary, you with your sanguine or melancholic personality. God's call is not uniform, which makes discerning it a true predicament of faith.

To consider the story of Moses, we see that it was his responsibility to God, and even to his own particularity, that he shouldered in the midst of great opposition. This man who meets God at Horeb, then receives the call to lead God's people out of Egypt, is the man who must withstand the people who want nothing of his specialness. In the book of Numbers we see enemies surface from within his own family: his brother, Aaron; his sister, Miriam. "Has the LORD indeed spoken only through Moses? Has he not spoken through us also?" Enemies surface from without: Korah, Dathan, Abiram, and the 250 chiefs of the congregation. "You have gone too far! For all in the congregation are holy, every one of them, and the LORD is among them. Why then do you exalt yourselves above the assembly of the LORD?" Moses had no greater intrinsic significance than any of the people, but he did have a particular calling from God, one that he had to exercise faithfully. That calling required a paradoxical degree of humility *and* self-assertion, which of course wasn't an assertion of himself so much as of the God who had made him and called him. "It is against the LORD that you and all your company have gathered together."

Like Moses, I want to stand fearlessly at the center of my story—God's story—like a strong live oak draped in Spanish moss. I no longer want to be tossed about by the weather of other people's expectations, by their imposed urgencies, by their strange confidences in *my* calling. I want, as an act of obedience, to account, with God's help, for where I am and who I am. If you will, I want to account for my specialness and feel that accounting, however paradoxically, to be part of my job of obedient faithfulness. I want a greening life, "to declare," with my own story, that "the LORD is upright; he is my rock, and there is no unrighteousness in him" (Ps 92:15). I want, like Amanda Berry Smith, to live fearlessly to glorify the sanctifying power of God. I can't live *your* life in glad and grateful response to God. In my body, I can only live my own.

It's a paradox that we could call out our specialness to the world—and also call it praise.

4

A WORD ABOUT GLORY

*B*efore he entered the corporate world in hopes of affording a college education for my brother and me, my father was a communications professor. He was always putting the two of us on a stage. At the end-of-year banquets for his debate team, we read from printed pages pulled from black leather folders. He had taught us to hold our bodies, to look at our audience, to use proper inflection. At the end of every performance, we were applauded for being children. I suppose you could say that I was set early by my father on the trajectory of public speaker.

Nevertheless, the first time I traveled to speak in more recent years, I stood in line at the airport Starbucks, a bundle of rankled nerves. In the snaking line of people, I became suddenly convinced that I had lost the passport I had just shown to the border control agent. Feverish minutes of frantic rifling through my bag finally produced it, but I was not to be calmed. Even now, after years of regular public speaking, with all the exterior calm I might muster, I have all manner of fears in standing in front of a crowd: fears that I'll lose my place in my notes, that I'll look ten pounds heavier on the screen behind me, that I haven't chosen the right shirt to pair with my blazer, that I'm wearing the wrong kind of shoes. The work of writing conceals me behind a page, but as a speaker on a platform I feel fatefully exposed. It takes prayer—urgent prayer—to put myself into such a public, scrutinizing gaze. Especially when I'm up after someone famous.

But these are the easiest fears to confess. There are other, less modest fears that I'm more loathe to tell you about: a fear, for instance, that I like the public speaking too much. Sometimes I will finish a talk and feel a rush of wonderment. On the one hand, I will have failed to recognize the person leaving the stage. And on the other, whoever she was, I will feel intensely proud of her.

Several years ago I enlisted the help of a spiritual director, intensely fearing the clutches of my own pride. I needed help to tamp down what centuries ago they called vainglory. I understood something of the inherently self-deceptive nature of pride, that it's smooth and sweet-talking, quick to see specks rather than logs. Writes C. S. Lewis, "There is one vice of which no man in the world is free; which everyone in the world loathes when he sees it in someone else; and of which hardly any people . . . ever imagine that they are guilty themselves."[1] Pride works by sleight of hand, and I haven't wanted to be caught in its web or cast in its spell.

But the surprise of these conversations with my spiritual director, Beth, hasn't been their confirmation of my desperately sin-sick soul. (That I'm depraved, of course, has never been in question.) The surprise has been that I've been forced to reexamine the nature of godly humility. As the paradox of the incarnation would have it, there is solace to be found in the word *and*.

As the paradox of the incarnation would have it, there is solace to be found in the word *and*.

▲ ● ■

My husband and I are learning, alongside our children, the recently published New City Catechism. The very first question sets out the most elemental commitment in Christian faith. "What is our only hope in life and death? That we are not our own but belong, body and soul, both in life and death, to God and to our Savior Jesus Christ."[2] The answer puts its finger squarely on the rebellious impulse of every human being: that we could forget the one to whom we owe all gratitude and worship and obedience. To be a sinner means to be a breaker of the very first commandment. Pride imperils us all.

It's our chronic temptation to displace God from his rightful place, and idolatry is part of our terminal disease called sin. My pastor recently told our small group his story of coming to faith in law school. After reading the Scriptures, a fair bit of C. S. Lewis, and Josh McDowell's *More Than a Carpenter*, Dan began to assent intellectually to the truths of Christianity. But he hadn't yet surrendered his life to Christ, which he realized when someone showed him a familiar tract. It included a picture of a throne. Rather than having Christ seated properly on that throne, the self has elbowed its way there. *High and mighty*, indeed. At that moment Dan realized what it would take, not just to believe in Jesus but to follow him. It would mean rightfully enthroning Christ at the center of his life—and dethroning whatever proud ambitions or desires or plans might compete.

The drift of our lives, says Sharon Miller, is toward self-focus. In her book *Free of Me*, she writes that we would make God about us, our appearance about us, our possessions about us, our friendships about us, our calling about us, our church about us. As corrupt human beings, we are the petulant sun, demanding that the stars and planets orbit around us. No wonder we must be vigilant about creeping pride. It's as if our hearts are baited—and pride waiting to bite.

We have every reason for self-suspicion. But maybe the answer to pride isn't just a quick self-forgetting fix. Maybe, as G. K. Chesterton suggests, Christian humility is poised on its own kind of paradox. "The average pagan, like the average agnostic, would merely say that he was content with himself, but not insolently self-satisfied, that there were many better and many worse. . . . In short, he would walk with his head in the air; but not necessarily with his nose in the air."[3] As Chesterton describes, a secular view of humility is one of moderation. It would have us practicing being neither too proud nor too humble, taking credit where credit is due without indulging too much applause. In this estimation, humility is neither white nor red; humility is a kind of *pink*.

Chesterton retorts: "[The church] has always had a healthy hatred of pink."[4]

He writes that Christian humility suggests something altogether more confounding than attenuated self-worth. Christian humility is both great *pride* as well as great *prostration*. On the one hand, we must recognize that we are the "chief of creatures," crowned with glory and honor, to quote the words of the psalmist. Unlike anything else in all of creation, we alone bear the image of God. In the beginning, "Man was a statue of God walking about in the garden."[5] And on the other hand, we must acknowledge that we are the "chief of sinners." We would greedily vie for all that is God's. Given the proverbial inch, we would take the fateful mile. The consistent testimony of Scripture is how good humans are at screwing things up.

It was pride that cast Satan into the lowest pit of hell, and this is a part of our story that we must tell. There's wariness to wear. But pride isn't the only part of the story. As the incarnation tells us, it is for glory that we are raised with Christ. "Let him call himself a fool and even a damned fool," writes Chesterton, "but he must not say that fools are not worth saving."[6]

▲ ● ■

In his book *On the Incarnation*, Athanasius puts forward the "dilemma" that God faced after the fall of humanity in the Garden. God told Adam and Eve that should they choose to eat the food that he had forbidden, they would surely die. When they did flout his command, he could not falsify himself by falsifying his word. Death was required for maintaining divine integrity. And yet, if God allowed his special creation, endowed with his own image, to fall into eternal disrepair, how could he call such apathy love? Could he be indifferent to the ruin of his own glory? No. "It was impossible . . . that God should leave man to be carried off by corruption, because it would be unfitting and unworthy of Himself."[7]

God solved the "divine dilemma" by sending his Son as a man, who would both pay the penalty for sin and reclaim humanity's glory. God solved the "divine dilemma" by sending his Son as a man, who would both pay the penalty for sin and reclaim humanity's glory. In the incarnation, God would be true to his word, true to his love, and true to his own glory.

In my own Southern Baptist tradition growing up, we thought a lot about the first part of God's redemptive work through Jesus. Because of the cross, we were saved from sin and death and hell. We were heaven-bound! But not much was to be made with the idea that Jesus was repairing the ruins of humanity's glory. Glory seemed always to be a word reserved for God. It was a fearful thing, as Herod learned, to try stealing glory from God (cf. Acts 12:20-23).

It *is* a fearful thing to try stealing glory from God. But what can be made of what Irenaeus has called the glory of a human being fully alive? What can be made of the glory of the chaste men and women and courageous martyrs who were God's burning bush in the time of Athanasius? "Who has ever so rid men of their natural passions that fornicators become chaste and murderers no longer wield the sword and those who formerly were craven cowards boldly play the man?"[8] What compelling witness does a transformed life have to offer to a watching world?

Athanasius observed how a commitment to following Jesus had produced in his disciples a radical sexual ethic, a radical desire for peace, a radical courage in the face of persecution. These chaste and courageous men and women were the very workmanship of God, a way of making his glory known in the world. And this was exactly as the incarnation had intended: "He, indeed, assumed humanity that we might become God."[9] The glory of *Christ in us* is God's glory indeed. Tim Keller has said we are more sinful and flawed than we ever dared believe, more loved and accepted in Jesus Christ than we ever dared hope. Might it also be true that in Jesus Christ we are more unimpressive than we ever dared admit, more glorious than we ever dared dream? What can be said through lives set alight? Are not the glorious children of God, alongside the rocks and the trees, the skies and the seas, taking up the chorus of Psalm 19 and pouring out the speech of God's praise: "Their voice goes out through all the earth, and their words to the end of the world."

To defer to a finer theological point, I'm talking of the doctrine of union with Christ—that in Christ, the old man and woman are baptized into death, a new man and woman raised to new life. It's from this position that true humility derives. Union with Christ is a doctrine, writes Rankin Wilbourne, that answers the question not what God has saved us *from* but what God has saved us *for*.

> Christ in you, by his Spirit, dwells and gives you new life and power to change. And all this happens without obliterating you as you. . . . You are more and more yourself when united to Christ. He covers you, he shields you, he represents you before the Father. He also fills you, illuminates you, and animates you, making you more yourself and more human than you could ever be on your own.[10]

Christ saves us *from* corruption and *for* glory. Lives set alight is part of the very purpose of God "who gave himself for us to redeem us from all lawlessness and to purify for himself a people for his own possession who are zealous for good works" (Titus 2:14).

By grace through faith, Christ, by his Spirit, takes up residence in our bodies, but he doesn't kick us to the curb. It is a Buddhist, not Christian, ideal that the self is obliterated and subsumed into God. To be sure there is a dying to self that is required before there can ever be a resurrection, and union with Christ requires a submission of this newly birthed self. We mortify all that is part of the old Eve and the old Adam: her jealousies and hatreds, his lusts and his disloyalties. But this surrender is not so that the self can be extinguished, only that it can burn most purely and radiantly. In other words, union with Christ requires I *and* he. *Holy* I, to be sure, but *I* nonetheless. Maybe union with Christ is why I can stand on a stage and do my own bit of modest marveling, why you can do whatever it is God is doing through you and feel, like Olympic runner Eric Liddell, the great pleasure of God. We don't recognize the *Christ is us* sometimes.

A candle stands at the center of our dining room table, and our family tries to remember to light it before dinner. Inevitably, someone will fight for the long-handled lighter, then ask for help when they can't work the two-part ignition mechanism. Someone will stick her fingers in the wax for the gooey feel between her fingers, accidentally dripping it on the table and putting the candle out. For such a simple chore, the lighting of this candle turns out to be a harrowing task.

God became flesh, bearing light into the world. And oh, the harrowing nature of the incarnation, which would aim to make glorious lights of us all: in our bodies, in our particular stories, in the ordinary landscape of our everyday. Too many public Christian figures have been scandalized by their pride, and it bears repeating that the millstones of their lives tie murderously around the necks of others. Pride is a slippery slope—but so is false humility. I can't imagine it pleases God any more to hang our heads and shuffle through life, mumbling apologies for our gifts and passions and looking at the floor. There is a proverbial bushel, and false humility would dangerously take cover under it. This is not the great, mysterious *and* of Christ in you.

With the Spirit's help, the dross of sin can be burned away that God's glory may shine even brighter in all of us. I don't know what good you're called to do in this world, but I do know that before the foundation of the world, you were called by the wonders of grace, blessed with every spiritual blessing in the heavenly place, even rescued from the clutches of your own pride. Keep falling into the strong, sure, and merciful hands of Jesus. And as you do, let your life burst into glorious flame. Be the bush that burns, bearing the image of God so brightly in the world that every man and woman must stop to remove their shoes and draw near for a closer look.

When they do, they'll see God.

QUESTIONS *for* REFLECTION *and* DISCUSSION

1. If you're a regular reader of the Bible, what kind of wondering tends to turn up in the pages of Scripture? What questions and curiosities persistently surface?

2. Of the four biblical paradoxes this book explores—incarnation, kingdom, grace, and lament—which have you thought most about? Which have you thought least about? Which makes you most curious and why?

3. Talk about your own personal experiences of walking by faith—and seeing through a glass darkly. When has God confounded your understanding? What surprises have you already had in your life with him?

4. What are the fruitful places of tension in your life right now, where the great I AND might be suggesting more creative alternatives than you have previously considered? How is your imagination stirred to follow him?

5. What spiritual practices might help you notice the annunciations of God in the everyday? Consider the practice of examen—the simple habit of reviewing the day with God—before you fall asleep at night.

6. If you began paying greater attention to the "specialness" of your own life, what might you discern about your calling? What do your circumstances, your passions, your abilities, and even your griefs, tell you about the way God wants to work through you for his glory?

7. How has false humility hindered God's work in and through you? How has pride? Choose an accountability partner, maybe even a spiritual director, to help you in the regular work of self-examination. Remember the great promise of the gospel: "It is God who works in you, both to will and to work for his good pleasure" (Phil 2:13).

8. What is the most helpful insight from this section on the incarnation? How will it help you to live differently in the kingdom of God?

PART TWO

KINGDOM

"Repent, for the kingdom of heaven is at hand." That's what Jesus announced at the launch of his public ministry as he proclaimed forgiveness of sins and pronounced healing over the blind, the lame, and the deaf. But for all his forthrightness, despite the fact the prophets had long foretold the coming of Israel's king, the kingdom itself was God's treasure hidden in a field. As N.T. Wright puts it in *How God Became King*, the paradox is this: "God acts completely unexpectedly— as he always said he would."

5

HIDING IN PLAIN SIGHT

*J*t only became a controversial prayer after the sermon, during the few minutes that are routinely devoted to Q&A. A tall, gray-haired man from the balcony waved his hand to catch our pastor's attention. He stood to mention the "young man's prayer" earlier in the service. (The young man was my forty-four-year-old husband.)

Ryan had prayed about the recent decision by an Ontario court to force provincial doctors, despite their conscientious objection, to provide referrals to patients wishing to die. (Physician-assisted death had been legalized by the Supreme Court of Canada one year earlier.) Ryan had prayed for the Christian doctors in our church and our city who were struggling to reconcile their Christian convictions with their legal obligations.

"I am personally very much in favor of physician-assisted death," the older gentleman in the balcony began. "I think this is a welcome turn in the modern world." He continued, "I'm just wondering: What role do personal politics have to play in the prayers prayed from the front? And how am I to pray along if I can't agree?" This man, a professor from the University of Toronto, had been visiting our church for a period of months, his spiritual search inspired by the younger woman seated beside him who had told him, "You need God."

"A wonderful question," our pastor began. "I'm so glad you've asked it.

"Maybe we could begin by considering the Christians in Nazi Germany who failed to defend the Jews. In hindsight, we can see that moral ambivalence proved to be the exactly wrong response. What the Christians of that day really needed was the moral courage to land squarely on the side of the Jews. It's only later, of course, that we can see this."

He continued, "There's no doubt that following Jesus will often put us on the 'wrong' side of our current cultural moment. People in the general culture will draw what they feel to be obvious conclusions, as in the case of PAD [physician-assisted death], but Christians, because of their theological commitments, won't draw those same conclusions." Though my pastor might not have adequately answered how we, in our differences, can pray together in unity, he went on to explain how theological commitments—such as the commitment to honor life, both at its beginning and end—necessarily inform our praying. Christians would not agree on every political issue, of course, but as a community, it was our job to wrestle with and work out the implications of Scripture in every aspect of life. It wouldn't do to make Christianity a matter of a private, personal affair—not when *the kingdom was at hand.*

To reflect on it later, the man's question seemed less to be about the nature of prayer and more about the nature of discipleship. He wanted to know, as we all want to know, just how much ground God intends to take in our lives. Is the kingdom of God the small patch of grass we safely cordon off on Sundays for our praying and kneeling, perhaps for our tossing a couple of coins in the plate as it's passed? The incarnation, of course, has already begun to answer that question for us. God means to lay exacting claim on our Monday through Saturday lives. When Jesus says follow, he doesn't just mean the hours before Sunday lunch.

"Repent, for the kingdom of heaven is at hand." That's what Jesus announced at the launch of his public ministry. After his baptism and forty days of temptation, when Jesus preached his first sermon, it was not, as we might imagine, a long exegetical trek through the Pentateuch or the prophets. Jesus did not quote Moses or Isaiah, even if the Gospel writers did so in their own biographies of Jesus' life. Rather, Jesus' first sermon was a simple one: a proclamation of God's at-hand kingdom. It was an announcement that situated him squarely in the Jewish hopes of first-century Roman-occupied Palestine, an announcement that eventually led to his arrest and execution. "King of the Jews" was the title that hung over the head of Jesus of Nazareth as he gasped his final breaths, crying out for the forgiveness of the guilty.

The announcement of the kingdom was not then—and is not now—the kind of announcement to abide indecision or indifference. It might be easier if kingdom faith were the stuff of private religious experience.

Easier still if the Sunday prayers of the kingdom ruffled no public feathers in the balcony.

▲ ● ■

Peter and Andrew, James and John first heard King Jesus' voice as they worked alongside their fathers, dragging in nets from the Sea of Galilee. I was also standing by a lake when I heard his call to follow. I was sixteen. I'd been raised by faithful Christian parents whose habit it was to take me and my brother to church three times weekly. In childhood, I was conversant in the essential doctrines of the Christian faith; at sixteen, I would have denied none of them. I'd been turned out by Vacation Bible School and Bible drills, by church choirs and Wednesday night prayer meetings. My favorite verses were Ephesians 2:8-9, which I had memorized in early elementary school from the KJV: "For by grace are ye saved through faith; and that not of yourselves: it is the gift of God: Not of works, lest any man should boast." But if I was a believer in Jesus at sixteen, I was no follower. I had another version of the good life, which included sleeping over at my boyfriend's house weekend nights when his parents were away. He too was raised in a Christian family, and we argued over the state of our salvation: I in favor, he against.

At sixteen, when I heard the voice of Jesus, I knew this much: that to follow him, I would be asked to turn from sexual sin. With God's help and by God's grace, I did that. But as I've come to understand it ever since, the kingdom doesn't just insist on the ethics of the bedroom; it upends every part of a human life. It's a deeper pool than we have imagined when we dive in. If the kingdom is good news, it surely isn't safe. Because there is no square inch of our lives that Jesus doesn't intend to rule.

If the kingdom is good news, it surely isn't safe.

It was a paradox, of course, that for all my faithful church attendance, for all my committed Bible memorization, for all my mastery of Christian belief, I was far from God and looking for love in all the wrong places. The kingdom was the elephant in the room—and I was missing it.

It seems I haven't been the only dense one. In his book *When God Became King*, N. T. Wright argues that *kingdom* is a theme we have largely ignored in the Bible. While we've tried being faithful readers of the Bible—paradoxically—we have often managed to miss its main point. "Creation, sin, Jesus. That is the implicit narrative of millions of Christians today—and it guarantees that they will never, ever understand either the Old Testament or the New."[1]

In other words, we've got our facts straight about the fall and our need for forgiveness. We understand that Jesus has died on the cross for our sins. But we don't really understand what God's up to beyond "getting us to heaven when we die." The gospel, with all its cosmic implications, is reduced to a simplistic formula like the one my own children learned to recite at another church's Vacation Bible School: *A*dmit that you're a sinner; *B*elieve that Jesus died for your sins; *C*onfess your faith in Jesus Christ as your personal Lord and Savior. As I told them then, that's leaving a lot of stuff out.

Yet despite our success in missing it, God's kingdom is the golden thread spun through Scripture from Genesis to Revelation. It's the radical idea of God's rightful rule over his people. At the very beginning, Eden was the kingdom of God on earth: God was King; humanity, subject. But tragically, those with whom God shared a certain degree of "rule" or dominion came by a wicked willfulness. They rejected his kingship and paid with their lives for their treason.

God renewed the kingdom project in the story of another man and his family, this time plucked from the hinterlands of Haran. "Go," God told Abraham, and "I will make of you a great nation" (Gen 12:1-2). The patriarch, becoming the progenitor of kings, would realize the kingdom as one scholar has summarized it,

"God's people in God's place under God's reign as a blessing to the nations."[2] His family would be a city set on the world's hill. They would blaze the light of God's kingdom.

But like the story of our first human parents, this story turns in its own woeful direction. Even though Moses and then Joshua, heirs of the Abrahamic promises, were appointed God's faithful rulers over his people, the land never fully became the possession of God's people. Like Adam, like Eve, Israel was a willful child. God's people rejected God's kingship, and their increasing appetite for conformity to other nations led to depths of moral depravity, social injustice, and spiritual rebellion. The united kingdom—under David, then Solomon—was just a two-generation memory when the kingdom splintered into factions of north and south. Israel's day darkened into bleaker, blacker night, and the people were eventually cast from God's land, brought back decades later to the ruin of Jerusalem and the temple. When the pages close on the Old Testament, there is a sense of bewildering loss. The people of God were asking this burning question after the prophets fell silent: If the kingdom is God's ultimate project, why is it always seeming to fail?

But the kingdom project did not fail in the waning years between the testaments. Rather, it was being prepared for the fullness of time when God would send his one-of-a-kind Son on a diplomatic mission to the overgrown garden of the world. This Jesus of Nazareth lives an important, often neglected, story in between the narrative poles of the creeds: "born of the virgin Mary" and "suffered under Pontius Pilate."[3] He preaches God's at-hand kingdom. Throughout his public ministry, he demonstrates his authority—as King—over demons and disease, even death itself. And what, of course, do the tenants of the garden do? They seize the Son to kill him, hoping to have his inheritance—which, by strange paradox of God's kingdom grace, demonstrated most fully on the cross, *they do.* When Jesus is raised three days later from the dead, it's clear that something has not ended but begun.

To read the story of Jesus in this way—as the fulfillment of the kingdom promised in the Old Testament—is to understand the scope of God's ambitions. He wills to reign. And he will reign over more than human *hearts.* The kingdom of God involves a reality much bigger than the private affairs of our lives, and it certainly stakes a claim bigger than individual salvation. To say that the kingdom of God is "at hand," to pray that the kingdom of God come "on earth as it is in heaven" isn't simply to call for new beliefs and new behaviors. It's to say that when the stone rolled away from the tomb and Jesus emerged from within, the upside-down world was turned right-side up.[4]

Kingdom prayers shake the pews. *And* kingdom lives shake the earth.

▲ ● ■

As with every part of God's story, there are surprises we turn up as we examine the kingdom. And one surprise according to the gospel writers, as I've been trying to explain it, is this: God's people almost missed it.

Paradoxically, God is a God who both self-reveals and hides. In the Old Testament we have many sightings of God, or *theophanies.* God visits Abraham before the destruction of Sodom and Gomorrah; he visits Jacob in the wilderness of Bethel and the ford of the Jabbok. Moses meets God in a bush that burns, sees God's back from the cleft of a rock. The cowardly Gideon meets the LORD and is strengthened for battle because of the visitation. The God of the Bible is a God who, because of his relentless love, relentlessly speaks to his people: in visions, in dreams, and face-to-face encounters, as with his servant Moses, whose face shone with divine afterglow. God speaks, and this self-revealing is fundamental to his character. He cannot *but* speak. (If only humans could *but* hear.)

According to one scholar, these Old Testament theophanies were both a veiling and an unveiling.[5] Willingly, God let himself be seen and heard, but he only let himself be seen and heard *partially*. When Moses requests a viewing of God's glory, God mercifully spares him his request. "You cannot see my face, for man shall not see me and live" (Ex 33:20). God hides Moses in the cleft of a rock, covers him with his hand, and allows the form of his goodness to pass by Moses. "Then I will take away my hand, and you shall see my back, but my face shall not be seen" (v. 23). God revealed himself—and also hid— because he loved his people. They longed to know him, but they could not "bear the sight of the divine glory in its plenitude."[6] Isaiah had understood this when, in a vision, he was caught up in the throne room of God. "Woe is me! For I am lost; for I am a man of unclean lips, and I dwell in the midst of a people of unclean lips; for my eyes have seen the King, the LORD of hosts!" (Is 6:5). Apart from God's merciful intervention, we are damned to see God.

Nevertheless, God becomes man and condescends to make himself fully known. But still, there is only partial recognition, at least for a little while. His disciples face bewilderment when the stone is rolled in front of the tomb. Although the story of Jesus is a clear continuation and fulfillment of the story of Israel, the Jews did not immediately understand it in this way. "The story reached its goal, but the story itself was looking in the wrong direction."[7]

The kingdom isn't simply plain truth; it's also mystery. Think of the befuddlement of the two disciples on the road to Emmaus (Lk 24). It was Easter morning, and the news of an empty tomb had not yet reached the travelers. Jesus found them looking sad, and as he fell in step beside them he played dumb when they talked of the weekend's headlines. "Are you the only visitor to Jerusalem who does not know the things that have happened there in these days?" They recounted the brutal events of Friday, when Jesus had been scandalously hung up on a cross, and confessed gloomily, "We had hoped that he was the one to redeem Israel."

> **The kingdom isn't simply plain truth; it's also mystery.**

"O foolish ones, and slow of heart to believe all that the prophets have spoken! Was it not necessary that the Christ should suffer these things and enter into his glory?" The kingdom, as Jesus would teach them, was never meant to bluster in like a bull. It had always been predicted to be carried in on a donkey—carried all the way to a cross.

6

BLESSED ARE

For as long as I knew her, her hands were old, her veins, thick as tree roots. For decades, clients arrived at the beauty shop at the front of her house on Arlington Street, and she shampooed them, cut them, and set them before sending them away.

"No one can shampoo your head like Aunt Pauline," my mom told my brother and me. Whenever we visited my great aunt in Akron, we would scramble onto one of her plastic chairs and whatever else she'd piled up to make us taller and allow her to tip our heads back into the bowl. The water, first cool, then warming, ran in rivulets down our scalps. She'd lather us up, and we'd wish the shampoo lasted longer—to prolong the massage, of course, but also to hear more macabre stories like the one of her brother drowning. As she told it, he'd been sweating and had jumped into an icy-cold creek.

My mother's paternal aunt was born in 1910 to poor parents in rural Kentucky. She had twelve brothers and sisters. When she was a young woman, she left the Kentucky fields for Akron, Ohio, to work at the Goodyear factory, and there she met and married Harry Carpenter. They never had children. As a child, I knew

Aunt Pauline to speak much of Jesus and little of Harry, who had died a relatively young man.

Aunt Pauline was always the relative to enliven a family party. While the rest of the adults sat sipping their lemonade, she'd jump up on a hot July day and get the kids "playing ball" in the front yard. She'd toss to us, miss when we tossed back, then chase the ball, now rolling toward the street, in her hitching kind of run. I see her put her knobby hand over her mouth. I hear her laugh at her clumsiness.

The house on Arlington Street stood three stories tall and smelled of cedar and rusty sinks. The Formica table in Aunt Pauline's kitchen, where we'd take our afternoon coffee together even when I was still a small child, was stacked with Bibles and devotional books and free notepads from the car mechanic. In those notepads she recorded reflections on Scripture and prayers to God. "Lord Jesus," those prayers always began. On the rare occasion that I spent the night at her house as a child, we'd sometimes lie awake in her bedroom as she recited Scripture aloud to fall asleep. She'd start with the A's: Ask, and you shall receive. B: Believe on the Lord Jesus Christ, and you shall be saved. C: Cast all your cares upon the Lord, for he cares for you. I see Aunt Pauline in her housecoat the next morning, smiling a gummy smile, that knobby hand over her mouth again. "Let me get my teeth in."

As I tell it to my children, Aunt Pauline was one of the live oaks spoken of in Psalm 92, who "flourish in the courts of our God. They still bear fruit in old age; they are ever full of sap and green." She ripened sweet with old age. She spent the final decades of her life as busily as she'd spent the earlier ones: not shampooing and setting hair, but volunteering at her local food pantry, attending church regularly, knitting lap blankets for people in the hospital. (After she moved out of the house on Arlington Street and into a retirement community, she added pool to this list of activities.)

Aunt Pauline was my flesh-and-blood Mother Teresa. Imagine my shock when, as a young woman, I sat on a squeaky upholstered rocker in her living room to hear her tell me about her abortion as a teenager. It had been the 1920s, the era of coat hangers and back-alley clinics. Before the pregnancy, she'd been naive about sex. After the abortion, she'd been naive about grief. I don't know why she told me that story that day, but I received it as her confession and have never told anyone until now.

Aunt Pauline died at ninety-three of a brain tumor. Mercifully, hers was a swift and relatively painless decline. If there were pearly gates that opened at her arrival, I imagine she ran through them in her hitching gait, laughing at whatever joke Saint Peter had prepared for her. Because if Aunt Pauline's life was not a glittering life . . .

It was surely a kingdom one.

▲ ● ■

Part of the paradox of the kingdom is that it should be so lavishly laid at the feet of those whom the world would call "least." When Jesus preached his famous Sermon on the Mount, he began by describing those who are blessed in the kingdom of God. Blessed are the poor in spirit. Blessed are the grieving. Blessed are the meek. As if to reverse expectations of who gets God's benediction, Jesus commends not the rich and the high-achieving, not the prim and the morally self-assured, but the Aunt Paulines of the world.

Take note of the blessed, Jesus preached, indicating the bedraggled crowd at his feet. Men and women had followed him from Galilee and the Decapolis, bringing along their sick and demon-possessed, their paralyzed and plagued. Look at the least, Jesus said, and see how much they are set to gain in God's kingdom. Although some preach the Beatitudes as a set of exacting religious criteria we must all meet, the point of the list is to say that "no one is beyond beatitude."[1] It doesn't matter the education you have or don't have, the salary you earn or don't earn, the squeaky-clean moral record you've kept or not kept. The kingdom is lavishly democratic in its blessing.

The kingdom, Dallas Willard puts it, tells us that improbable people are "riotously celebrated in the party of Jesus."[2] There is, as one example, Matthew, the tax collector Jesus calls to follow

> The kingdom is lavishly democratic in its blessing.

him. Rising up from his tax booth, Matthew throws a lavish party in honor of his new master, and the Pharisees are decidedly disapproving of the guest list. Matthew has invited his colleagues and other "sinners." The Pharisees ask Jesus' disciples, "Why does your teacher eat with tax collectors and sinners?" They were expecting that anyone proclaiming God's at-hand kingdom might have been more careful to keep better company. But Jesus is emphatic about the kingdom's purpose: "Those who are well have no need of a physician, but those who are sick" (Mt 9:12). In other words, the promise of God's kingdom is neither for the self-sufficient nor the morally upright but for the needy and the reprobate. It's the coughing frail who get in first.

As another example of improbable people riotously celebrated in the kingdom, there is the sinful woman who washes Jesus' feet with her tears and wipes them with her hair. She unpins her locks, radiant blackness falling past her shoulders, and we can almost hear the crowd gasp at the sensuous act, the scent of her spilled perfume filling the air. Simon, a Pharisee, and Jesus' host, reasons that Jesus cannot be a prophet else "he would have known who and what sort of woman this is who is touching him, for she is a sinner" (Lk 7:39). As Simon concludes, the only proper response of a holy man to such a woman would be to recoil.

Jesus' reputation as a holy man is constantly scandalized by touch. The leper, the bleeding woman, the blind, and the dead: Jesus touches and allows himself to be touched. The at-hand kingdom isn't distant or removed, cordoned off from impurity. It's walking among the crowds, and they are reaching for the hem of his robe. Even the disciples fail to keep Jesus from the touch of the sticky children, whose parents clamor to get them in his lap as if he's Santa at the local mall. "Let the little children come to me and do not hinder them, for to such belongs the kingdom of heaven."

Who would believe that front-row seats are reserved for such as these?

Forgotten is a word that Allen uses to describe himself when I speak with him by phone. "You're easy to talk to," he tells me after fifteen minutes. "And you're easy to talk to," I tell him. We agree to meet at the open-house event that our church is hosting where his portrait will hang in our main-floor gallery. He promises to bring me samples of his work, and I promise to make time to look at them.

As we chat, I learn that Allen describes himself as the "disability photographer" of the marginalized neighborhood into which our church has recently moved. "I am the photographer of the forgotten," Allen tells me over the phone. "Because I am one of the forgotten." He describes being hearing impaired, tells me about suffering a traumatic brain injury, admits that he is poor. His art, he says, isn't a passion but "a way of surviving." As we speak, I think of the photograph of Allen that will hang in the main hall of our church: keen eyes and bushy eyebrows, a camera slung around his neck and a red poppy pinned to his shirt.

Who but the forgotten get their portraits hung in the kingdom of God?

▲ ● ■

Yet I am not one of the forgotten—and neither are most members of my downtown Toronto church. By comparison to Aunt Pauline, to Allen, and to the men and women keeping warm winter days inside the Horticultural Pavilion in our church's backyard, we lead glittering kinds of lives. Lawyers, doctors, corporate executives, we are the degreed and the titled, the high-achieving and the partnered. Able-bodied, we are paying mortgages, affording vacations, and saving for retirement. Maybe the paradox of the kingdom is not just that it can be enjoyed by the poor and the forgotten but that it could also belong to the rich and comfortable. I am bewildered to think that God's embrace is big enough for big britches like us.

The kingdom of God is, without question, a revolutionary movement. And revolutionary movements are often accompanied by intense hatred for those at the top of society's status ladder. In the late nineteenth century, royal heads rolled in revolutionary France when the Bastille was stormed and Versailles surrounded, the people ridding themselves of their cake-eating king and queen. In 1917, Russia had overturned its own aristocracy, establishing a government with proletariat interests. For the next seventy-odd years, communism was anchored in the revolutionary promise of exacting equality. How many entries in our history books quench the thirst for justice with the reversal of fortunes? We are eager to witness Humpty Dumpty fall—happier still if he's the king.

In more recent news headlines, we see our continuing interest in favoring the poor over the rich, the weak over the powerful. Whether it's Dominique Strauss-Kahn, a powerful French politician, and a hotel maid at a Manhattan hotel, or Harvey Weinstein and an up-and-coming actress, we feel a certain degree of smug satisfaction when the high and mighty get their due. I have, of course, zero interest in defending either of these men or others like them, who egregiously abuse their power, nor do I wish to say that we shouldn't examine and change the structures of oppression in our society that disenfranchise the poor and marginalized. But what am I trying to unearth is the *surprise* we should feel that the kingdom should have room for the political elite, for the Hollywood film mogul (even a criminal one), and every McMansion-owning, middle-level manager in between.

Though Jesus hails from a small corner of the Roman empire, though most of his ragtag band of followers are equally unimpressive, though the poor and disenfranchised are those most hungry and thirsty for righteousness, this doesn't preclude wealthy women from underwriting his ministry expenses (Lk 8:1-3) and the well-resourced Joseph of Arimathea from burying Jesus' body in his own family crypt (Jn 19:38-42). The kingdom of God is even making room for such as these.

There are, of course, obvious material implications of this kingdom news, and Jesus minces no words in the Sermon on the Mount: we cannot serve both God and money. It's also true that getting the rich into the kingdom of heaven will require the miraculous intervention of God himself (Mt 19:24-26). Jesus speaks hard words to the rich young ruler who wishes to secure his standing with God: "If you would be perfect, go, sell what you possess and give to the poor, and you will have treasure in heaven; and come, follow me" (Mt 19:21). Jesus will not allow someone's money or status to keep them from following him wholeheartedly: *but he loves them nonetheless.*

Even in the Gospel of Luke, where there's frequent censure of the wealthy, we still have glimmers of hope for camels trying to pass through the gospel needle's eye even if Luke is certainly interested in the gospel's ability to reverse fortunes. In Luke's Gospel, Mary sings her Magnificat, which proclaims her story of divine favor: "He has filled the hungry with good things, and the rich he has sent away empty" (Lk 1:53). Luke is also the only Gospel writer to record the haunting parable of the rich man and Lazarus: "Remember that you in your lifetime received your good things, and Lazarus in like manner bad things; but now he is comforted here, and you are in anguish" (Lk 16:25). Further, Luke's Beatitudes, unlike Matthew's, are followed by woes: Woe to you who are rich; woe to you who are full now.

But lest we think that there's no room for the rich at God's table, we also find in the Gospel of Luke the story of a wee little rich man invited to dine with Jesus. It wasn't simply that Zacchaeus had gotten rich because Daddy left him the family carpet-cleaning business. Zacchaeus was a greedy tax collector, despised by his countrymen for the illicit profits he made off their backs. Jesus invites himself to the house of this rich man, and when Zacchaeus publicly repents of his corruption, Jesus joyfully announces, "Today salvation has come to this house, since he also is a son of Abraham. For the Son of Man came to seek and to save the lost" (Lk 19:9-10). It's a surprise that the kingdom has generous room for the least— a paradox that it welcomes those with much.

It's a surprise   Thascius Cyprian was a wealthy, urbane
that the kingdom   aristocrat from Carthage when he became a
has generous   Christian in the middle of the third century.
room for the   After his conversion, he worried to a friend in
least—a paradox   a letter that he, a rich man, might be unable to
that it welcomes   enter the kingdom of heaven. "Could he be
those with much.   liberated from a world that he found both se-
ductive and oppressive? Could someone who 'has been used to
liberal banquets and sumptuous feasts . . . learn thrift'? Could he be
content with 'ordinary and simple clothing' or find happiness without
the buzz of fawning supplicants?"[3] But in Pontius's *Life of Cyprian*,
it's well-attested that Cyprian became earnestly committed to the
poor and "gave away a substantial portion of his inherited estates for
their relief."[4] Even a rich man can learn to seek first the kingdom.

Maybe the paradox of the kingdom isn't simply that it liberally
comes to everyone who would receive it, rich or poor. Maybe its
best surprise is that it would come at the behest of a seeking and
saving God. What's clear about the good news of the kingdom is
that whomever it finds, they likely haven't been looking for it. They
were about their ordinary lives, dragging in fish to sell at the market,
shampooing a neighbor's head, and sleeping over at their boyfriend's house. Then Jesus strides by, calling out the good news of
a new (or maybe old) way of being in the world. Repent, for the
kingdom of God is at hand.

We can't know everything that means, but by faith, we follow
this Jesus, falling in step behind him. Because the thought of flying
right-side up sure sounds good.

7

BIRDS AND BARNS

*W*e will leave next week for Iceland, then Malta. It will not be news that I announce on Facebook. Once a year, Ryan's work as an executive takes us to exotic locations like the westernmost point of Portugal, dangling us from a luxurious perch over the glittering ocean and feeding us over several courses. It is never public news. The silence is not to protect our children whom we've left home with Grandma, although I suppose that would be a good caution to exercise. Instead, the silence is entirely self-protective. I fear someone will suspect that this dressed-up life at Michelin-starred restaurants, even if just stretched over the span of a week, is not a kingdom life.

I had prescient hesitations before marrying Ryan, a long-haired business and economics major now sitting in the C-Suite of a Fortune 500 company. Wholly committed to Jesus, at twenty-two he was not committed to full-time ministry. I, on the other hand, was studying to be a teacher and planning to give my "everything" to Jesus, imagining it would lead me to a life of singleness and missionary service. Reading the biographies of Amy Carmichael, of Helen Roseveare, of Darlene Deibler Rose, I thrilled at the

unadulterated devotion of these women, anticipated my own dis-
appearance in some remote corner of India or the Congo or Papua
New Guinea. It was their heroism I coveted; it was their degree of
specialness in the kingdom of God that I clamored after.

Elisabeth Elliot, the wife of martyred missionary Jim Elliot,
who returned to Ecuador with their young daughter after her husband's brutal murder, had been a resident of Williston dorm at
Wheaton College, the same dorm I moved into the winter of my
junior year after returning from a semester abroad. I lay in my top
bunk, imagining this to be the very room where she'd penned some
of her most fervent prayers to God. From the third floor, I tried
breathing in her valor, her surrender; at the age of twenty, I tried
gaining something of her uncompromising faith.

Jim and Elisabeth Elliot's names, among many others, hang
along a wall at Blanchard Hall, the stately limestone building
that stands at the highest point of Wheaton's campus. The names
of these devoted students, flung far into the world for Christ,
some never to return, are cataloged by year of graduation. The
wall proves that their lives have mattered, that they have been
sufficiently poured out on the altar as they counted everything
as "rubbish" compared to the infinite value of knowing Christ
and making him known. As an undergraduate, even as a woman
returning twenty years after my graduation, I have urgently
wanted my name on that wall—in part, because I'm that desperate for approval, in part because it hasn't ever been hard to
imagine the massive ledger that God must be keeping in heaven.
Brow furrowed, pencil sharpened, he is, as I've often seen him,
bent over the numbers—the sacrifices, the salaries—weighing
human lives to calculate their kingdom contribution. To have

your name on the wall, you could be assured that your account with God was in the black.

Kingdom lives, I have often assumed, must necessarily follow a narrative of gloomy sobriety—like that of Aiden W. Tozer, who married his wife, Ada Pfautz, when they were both young. Lacking a seminary education, Tozer aspired to be a preacher, and many considered him to be specially anointed by God. On the day of his ordination to the ministry, he determined to resign all selfish ambition and greedy desire. "Save me from the bondage to things. Let me not waste my days puttering around the house. . . . Deliver me from overeating and late sleeping. Teach me self-discipline that I may be a good soldier of Jesus Christ."[1] Tozer's devotional life was characterized by rigid fervency. As Karen Wright Marsh describes in her book *Vintage Sinners and Saints*, he spent hours in his prayer closet, lying prostrate before the Lord. His was an otherworldly life, as he described it should be in *The Pursuit of God*. "If we truly want to follow God, we must seek to be other-worldly. . . . Every man must choose his world."[2]

But if Tozer's "other-worldliness" seems heroic, as Marsh describes in her book, his exacting life of faith came at great cost to his family. Aside from the financial strain he caused them by foreswearing profits from his books and giving away half his salary, his children remembered him, after his death, as distant and disengaged. His wife, remarrying after his death, said, "I have never been happier in my life. Aiden loved Jesus Christ, but [my second husband] loves me."[3]

In contrast to Tozer's ascetic life, however, Dietrich Bonhoeffer's early life as a child, adolescent, and young man was a relatively pampered one. As biographer Charles Marsh describes him, born to upper-middle-class German parents, Bonhoeffer was a bit of a dandy, writing away to his mother from his first ministry position with requests to send clothes. Bonhoeffer had never known want, only relative privilege. He was well-educated, well-traveled. When he started a seminary for the Confessing Church (the movement of churches during World War II that did not join the pro-Nazi Protestant Reich Church), it was furnished by a patron with dueling grand pianos, and it was at the piano that Bonhoeffer could fall into excited, even frightening fits of ecstasy. Bonhoeffer was a man who could preach a rousing sermon; he was also a man to appreciate a night at the opera. Even from prison, he was writing to his family, asking for better clothes.

In Scripture we have fierce and frowning men like Tozer—men like John the Baptist. John arrived on the scene with his camel-hair cloak and leather belt. He stood on the periphery of society, eating locusts and wild honey and calling down the brimstone of God's judgment. "For John came neither eating nor drinking, and they say, 'He has a demon'" (Mt 11:18). John's crime was belonging too little to this world; his fault was his otherness, his set-apartness. This lone voice crying out in the wilderness makes few friends as he baptizes men and women in the river Jordan. "You brood of vipers! Who warned you to flee from the wrath to come?" (Mt 3:7).

Jesus was not one of those fierce and frowning men. It is curious to me that John the Baptist was accused of being too heavenly-minded, Jesus too earthly-minded. Surely Jesus, Son of God, would not keep company with revelers—would not himself be one. But in contrast to his cousin, Jesus of Nazareth was a regular guest at parties and a regular host at his own table. He lacked the expected asceticism and was considered by the religious leaders of his day as being too much of the world. His first miracle, of course, was providing the wine for local wedding festivities. "The Son of Man came eating and drinking, and they say, 'Look at him! A glutton and a drunkard, a friend of tax collectors and sinners!'" (Mt 11:19).

It's the stories of Tozer and Bonhoeffer, John the Baptist and Jesus, that keep me wondering: What is the shape of a kingdom life? Just how worldly—or how ascetic—is it? Paradoxically, I seem to be offered examples of both kinds of lives, which leaves me with more wondering. Am I meant to be Tozer, wearing out the knees of my pants and refusing proceeds from the sale of my books? Or am I meant to be Bonhoeffer, seeing no inherent crisis in privilege and obedience? Am I better off to imitate the stern faith of John the Baptist, whose name most surely made it on the wall of God? Or can I, like Jesus, indulge an eating and drinking faith without fearing the wrath of the ledger-keeper?

In other words, is it possible to die for God and worry for the state of one's shoes while climbing the scaffold?

▲ ● ■

My writer friend Christina says we would have made good nuns. She speaks with a kind of wistfulness about the celibate vocations, which isn't to say that she or I wish life were different so much as we long that life fractured less between morning carpool, book deadlines, and afternoon pickup, to say nothing of piano lessons and basketball tournaments. Our domestic roles, however much we cherish them, make us subject to constant demand and constant interruption—this, no matter how early we get up. There are thoughts to think and prayers to pray—and the dryer is always dinging.

But it's not just that I long for a quieter life; I long for a more guiltless one. I imagine myself clothed in one of my two black habits, kneeling at prayer. Dedicated fully to God, I no longer pay a mortgage or pay to color my hair. I am divested of my worldly possessions and every self-recriminating thought of selfishness and greed. I am Thérèse of Lisieux, praying fervently to God: "My God, I choose all! I do not wish to be a saint by halves."[4] I imagine the *either* of the nunnery sparing me the *or* of the world.

But it is a fantasy that bursts like a bubble the moment I open the budget spreadsheet on my computer. I am not a nun, wearing out her knees on the cold stone floor of a convent. Instead, it's the week for deciding on the contractor we'll hire to renovate the house.

In the book of 1 Timothy, Paul offers words of paradox for the rich of the world seeking to live kingdom lives. His words are not, as some suppose, the *and* that many of us so feverishly cherish, plying us with the lie that we can serve the kingdom of God *and* our 401(k)s. No, Jesus has already fiercely dispelled that rumor: "No one can serve two masters, for either he will hate the one and love the other, or he will be devoted to the one and despise the other. You cannot serve God and money" (Lk 16:13). Like Jesus, Paul warns the members of the Ephesian church about the seduction of money and the apostasy on the other side of greed, writing, "Those who desire to be rich fall into temptation, into a snare, into many senseless and harmful desires that plunge people into ruin and destruction." The almighty dollar, Paul writes, is a sword on which any of us might fall: "It is through this craving [to be rich] that some have wandered away from the faith and pierced themselves with many pangs" (1 Tim 6:9, 10). To make wealth an unequivocal blessing from God is to miss the truth of Scripture; money can indeed be a curse.

I don't want to foolishly say that the rich are the blessed, that the prospered are the divinely favored. But I do want to say that the rich and the prospered, in God's kingdom, have a much greater responsibility than apologies for their privilege. If I have sought *eithers* and *ors* in my kingdom calling, it has often been to assuage my guilt for my privilege. But Paul, writing to Timothy, pastor of the Ephesian church, seems to have no consideration for my beleaguered conscience. He writes,

> As for the rich in this present age, charge them not to be haughty, nor to set their hopes on the uncertainty of riches, but on God, who richly provides us with everything to enjoy. They are to do good, to be rich in good works, to be generous and ready to share, thus storing up treasure for themselves as a good foundation for the future, so that they may take hold of that which is truly life. (1 Tim 6:17-19)

I want Paul to tell me to sell everything and follow Jesus, but he refuses such ultimatums, even if he will not let me indulge excess, even if he will insist on radical generosity.

In the kingdom of God, I am paradoxically called to give *and* to enjoy.

As cure for the love of money, Paul does not commend an ascetic life. Earlier in 1 Timothy 4, he has

In the kingdom of God, I am paradoxically called to give *and* to enjoy.

in fact called out the false teachers in the Ephesian church who have forbidden marriage and the eating of certain kinds of food. Asceticism of this sort is not holiness, Paul writes. "Everything created by God is good, and nothing is to be rejected if it is received with thanksgiving, for it is made holy by the word of God and prayer" (vv. 4-5). Paul returns to similar themes of enjoyment and gratitude that we read in our discussion of the incarnation. The material gifts God provides need not be a source of shame, even if they must be handled with great caution. There is temptation to pride in wealth. There is a false hope we could derive from our perceived financial security. Our money can, in real ways, displace our trust in God. Do not hear me say that we get to serve the kingdom of God and mammon.

Paul tells Timothy to ensure that the wealthy people in his congregation are living the right story of the good life—not the story whose version Paul gives in 1 Corinthians 15:32: "If the dead are not raised, 'Let us eat and drink, for tomorrow we die.'" To live a kingdom life is not to gorge on every pleasure offered today. There's a better story to live, and to live the story of God's kingdom has implications from what we do with every dollar passing through our hands. Do great good in this world, writes Paul. Serve and share, remembering that every "sacrifice" is an investment in the life to come. Give and give away in order to "take hold of that which is truly life" (1 Tim 6:19). Own everything loosely: because anything can be lost or needed by another.

The Dow Jones doesn't decide our future: ours is an otherworldly hope, a hope often measured by the willingness to do without.

I know people who live this hope well; none would wish to be named. I think of the couple that moved back from Europe after their banking careers had secured a comfortable financial future for themselves. When they returned to the United States, they didn't buy the large, beautiful suburban home they could have easily afforded. Instead, they paid cash for a small Cape Cod house and invested the rest of their savings in a small Christian school they started together, both working for years without salaries. They live the secretive life of the kingdom, hardly letting their right hand know of their left hand's generosity.

It's my secret too: what we have and give away. But I'm learning this much: if generosity is at the heart of God's work in the world, paradoxically, so is gladness. I hope we'll learn to live the kind of radically generous, radically carefree earthly lives that the kingdom inspires us to. Not because there's a wall and a roster of names, not because there's a ledger-keeper but because we follow a radically generous God who became poor for our sakes. I hope we'll guilt-lessly seek first God's kingdom coming, knowing there's nothing we need worry after, nothing we need secure for ourselves, nothing we need prove or earn or hoard. I hope we'll invest zealously in the life to come, knowing there are no rights we can't give up, no en-titlements we can't abandon. I hope we'll remember that God's clothing the lilies of the field and feeding the birds of the air.

I hope we'll remember that barns, even renovated ones, never lasted into eternity anyways.

8

THE HIGH TREASON
OF HALLELUJAH

*T*he organizers were skittish about the women's retreat they
had invited me to lead. "We just want unity," they told me
in multiple nervous conversations over the phone in the weeks
leading up to the event. After the 2016 election, divisions had
emerged in their congregation, as it had in many other evangelical
churches across the United States. On the Sunday after Donald
Trump's unexpected victory, their pastor addressed the people
standing along the fault lines, and on both sides of the divide,
people stood to leave, affronted either by what he'd said or left
unsaid. In the months to follow, the pastor would be simultaneously
criticized for silence and for speaking out on issues like border
control and foreign policy. "You don't intend to talk about politics,
do you?" the retreat organizers wanted to be assured, knowing that
I'd be teaching from the book of Ruth, a story of immigrant faith.

Ironically, on the day of my departure for the retreat, I opened
the paper to read this headline: "Evangelicals, Having Backed
Trump, Find White House 'Front Door is Open.'"[1] The article
featured a picture of evangelical leaders gathered around President

Trump in the Oval Office, laying hands on him to pray. The Reverend Jonnie Moore, the thirty-four-year-old Southern Baptist minister who had been a co-chairman of the Trump campaign's evangelical advisory board, had posted the picture on Twitter six months after Trump's inauguration with this caption: "Such an honor to pray within the Oval Office for @POTUS and @VP."

On the one hand, the picture might have simply illustrated these leaders' obedience to the instructions Paul gave to Timothy: "I urge that supplications, prayers, intercessions, and thanksgivings be made for all people, for kings and all who are in high positions" (1 Tim 2:1-2). On the other, it may have signaled something much more nefarious, picturing the kind of corruption Michael Gerson cites in his April 2018 cover article for *The Atlantic*. Gerson writes, "The moral convictions of many evangelical leaders have become a function of their partisan identification. . . . Blinded by political tribalism and hatred for their political opponents, these leaders can't see how they are undermining the causes to which they once dedicated their lives." As many are asking, Have American evangelicals conflated loyalty to God with loyalty to party?

The kingdom of God is not painted in red or blue. Neither Republicans nor Democrats have their pulse on the kingdom of God, and for that matter the kingdom does not grow because of political influence and social clout. In fact, as Scripture makes clear, God's kingdom is frequently in conflict with the pharaohs and caesars of its day. Paradoxically, the kingdom of God seems to have all the vulnerability—and virulence—of a little seed. Even more surprising, the only way that this seed is ultimately harvested is through suffering. Unless a grain of wheat falls into the earth and dies, Jesus said. God's holy hill isn't Capitol Hill but Golgotha.

▲ ● ■

We turn the pages to the New Testament and immediately understood that God's at-hand kingdom has its enemies. To begin

God's holy hill isn't Capitol Hill but Golgotha.
with Matthew's Gospel is to meet Herod the Great, who years earlier has been crowned "King of the Jews" by the Roman Senate. When the wise men show up on the scene to ask about the whereabouts of a new "king of the Jews," a king whose star they've been following, Herod understands, trembling, that a rival has been born.

Herod's kingdom is like every earthly kingdom: it's only as strong as its will to self-protect. Herod sees a political threat and aims to put it to death. News of a rival king of the Jews incites Herod to murder, and he wages cruel war on all the male children in Bethlehem and the surrounding region. Nevertheless, an invisible force is at work against Herod the not-so-Great. First, in a dream, the wise men are warned to return to their country by another way. Second, Joseph is warned to take his new wife and newborn son and flee to Egypt. All the political and military might in the world crumbles when the divine will blows in the opening of Matthew's Gospel. People sleep, and God acts, his wind placing Jesus at safe distance from a megalomaniacal king. Then, with a kind of abrupt narrative curtness, Matthew tells us just how much to fear Herod and political leaders like him: "When Herod died" (Mt 2:19). Earthly kings have expiration dates. They are mere footnotes in the bigger story that God's writing.

The impotence of earthly kingdoms in contrast to the power of God's at-hand kingdom is similarly illustrated in Matthew 14.

Herod Antipas, Herod's son, is now ruling in his dead father's place, and he hears of this man, Jesus, purported to be exercising miraculous powers. Paying close attention to the text, we'll see that Herod's first assumption about Jesus' identity is the most improbable one: "This is John the Baptist. He has been raised from the dead; that is why these miraculous powers are at work in him" (Mt 14:2). Surely this is not the first logical conclusion to draw—except, of course, if you have the irrepressible hunch that God's kingdom always wins, despite your best efforts to snuff it out.

For all his Roman support, Herod Antipas seems to have intimations of his own powerlessness—certainly the powerlessness of the edge of his sword. His lesson was pharaoh's lesson many centuries earlier, a story which Rahab the prostitute knew how to tell:

> We have heard how the LORD dried up the water of the Red Sea before you when you came out of Egypt, and what you did to the two kings of the Amorites who were beyond the Jordan, to Sihon and Og, whom you devoted to destruction. And as soon as we heard it, our hearts melted, and there was no spirit left in any man because of you, for the LORD your God, he is God in the heavens above and on the earth beneath. (Josh 2:10-11)

God has no hesitation about making himself famous.

If the kingdom of God could be established by political alliances, we would see an entirely different story playing out in the Gospels. Jesus would certainly not have begun his public ministry in the West Virginia of his day, which is to say, Galilee. He would have emerged under the brighter lights of Manhattan or Washington, DC—of Jerusalem or Rome. He would have made sure to position himself for the right kinds of networking opportunities, made sure to hobnob with the right kinds of people. Instead, as the Gospel writer John makes clear in his Gospel, Jesus is dodging in and out of Jerusalem with the infuriating desire to remain a hidden figure. Even his brothers grow exasperated by his furtive movements: "Leave here and go to Judea, that your disciples also may see the works you are doing. For no one works in secret if he seeks to be known openly. If you do these things, show yourself to the world" (Jn 7:3-4). Whatever Jesus is up to, it's not from the playbook of "How to Win Friends and Influence People." And ironically, when he does finally resolve to go to Jerusalem, he tells his friends that it is to go to his death.

Although his disciples weren't quick to understand this, Jesus tried telling them that his kingdom would upend their expectations. My followers aren't bearers of the sword, he declared. Rather, they carry a cross. And do not expect that we will take kingdom power by force or by popular will. Rather, we'll be delivered over to courts and flogged in the synagogues. "You will be hated by all for my name's sake" (Mt 10:22). Jesus promised his disciples no victory in the local popularity contest. Instead, he promised persecution. He promised suffering. As N. T. Wright has written, "Sharing his suffering is the way in which [we] are to extend his kingdom in this world."[2]

An appetite for worldly power can lead us to embrace the truth of the kingdom but reject its way.[3] Are not the stories of the murderous Pharaoh, drowning God's babies in the Nile, and the genocidal Herod, strangling the breath of Bethlehem boys, a warning to exercise wariness when it comes to pledging our allegiance to political figures? What lessons are we to learn from Jesus himself, who standing before Pilate admitted, "My kingdom is not of this world. If my kingdom were of this world, my servants would have been fighting, that I might not be delivered over to the Jews" (Jn 18:36)? What fear and trembling should we have to hear the leading priests' admission, at the time of Jesus' arrest and bogus trial, that "we have no king but Caesar"?

In more recent history, what lessons might we learn from the German National Church during World War II, which so easily ceded its conscience for the sake of power? They had no king but Hitler. I am all for praying for our president, but I do not support bedding down with him, no matter his political party, not least when his manner of speaking and behaving betrays utter disregard for the values of the kingdom.

The kingdom of God doesn't grow in ways we expect. In fact, as Jesus describes in many parables, one of the paradoxes of the kingdom is its seeming *vulnerability*. It's a handful of seeds scattered along the ground, most of which are either eaten by birds, withered by drought, or choked by thorns. Only the rare few grow to harvest. It's a treasure hidden in a field, nearly missed by the careless traveler on his hurried, merry way. It's one pearl of great price—not, as much as we might like it to be, an entire wheelbarrow full.

The kingdom of God is not accompanied by brass bands, not built by

> One of the paradoxes of the kingdom is its seeming *vulnerability*.

dramatic gestures of grandeur. Its center of operations is not the Oval Office. Rather, the kingdom of God is something to miss and neglect, something seemingly endangered and threatened. Like Herod Antipas, we know God's kingdom wins—but it sure doesn't win according to the rules of winning. There is no greater example of this than our crucified Savior, strung up for public mockery, his death a stone of stumbling for those seeking a different kind of power and a different kind of wisdom.

As Jesus faced Pilate in the remaining hours of his life, he was clear about the power dynamics of God's kingdom. "You would have no authority over me at all unless it had been given you from above" (Jn 19:11). Pilate—and the Jewish leaders and Roman soldiers—did not take Jesus' life; he handed it over willingly. To say that Jesus is King is to say that every authority derives from him and submits to him.

That confession of faith has been and will continue to be an act of subversion.

▲ ● ■

We don't vote the kingdom into office; we live its compelling hope every day. To understand what that hopeful, daily living means, N. T. Wright commends the example of faithful first-century Jews, living the reality of exile, as a model for our imitation: "They were able to develop a theological account of the comings and goings of pagan nations and their rulers as well as a subversive literature and lifestyle designed to critique the pagan rulers, to encourage the faithful, and to warn of God's ultimate judgment."[4] In other words, the Jews never invested their hope fully in any one political leader. They understood the psalmist when he wrote that "He who sits in the heavens laughs; the Lord holds [the kings of the earth] in derision" (Ps 2:4). Exiled Jews worked to tell the right story and to live subversively in light of it.

The stories we tell shape the lives we lead. The subversive literature of first-century Jews was, of course, the writings of the prophets, which told them that God would not abandon them but would return to them as King. Even if these Jews were under Roman rule, they did not give up believing that God would make good on his promises to his people, that a day of reckoning was coming, that justice would be finally served for the faithful. The story they told was as simple as this: God made the world, and he would redeem it. And because they told that story, their lifestyle was also subversive, not least because they kept Sabbath. If, like them, we're reading the subversive literature of the Bible—with all its proclamations of God's kingdom coming to earth as in heaven—like first-century Jews, we're meant to be living subversively.

A kingdom life is always a nonconforming life, and subversion is a form of witness.

It seems clear from scholarly research that the growth of the early church was not owed to clever and compelling evangelistic strategies. Believers did not go door to door handing out tracts. They did not hold open-air revival meetings, preaching the Word and asking people to walk the aisle and repent of their sins. According to Alan Kreider's *The Patient Ferment of the Early Church*, Christians lived distinctively, and those differences testified to the truth of the gospel.

Specifically, the efforts of "catechism" or spiritual formation in the early church focused on four specific areas of subversive Christian lifestyle: sexual chastity, financial stewardship and simplicity, abandonment of the magic arts, and patience (in contrast to hatred and violence). I wonder about our own acts of subversion as we try living faithfully in each of these areas today. What credible public witness might be restored to the church, not because we showed up to cast a ballot for a particular party or president, but simply because we committed to living virtuously in each of these four areas?

In a culture driven by identity politics, it is subversive to reject the idea that our primary identity is our sexual identity. In our now gender-fluid world, it is subversive to say that bodies matter. So long as opinion pieces are published by porn stars in the *New York Times*, arguing that we have no right to "dictate the way adult performers have sex with one another, or what is good and normal, aside from requiring that it be consensual," it will continue to be subversive to say that porn is wrong and consent too watery a standard to decide questions of sexual ethics. So long as personal freedom remains our highest ethic, it will be increasingly subversive to say that sex exclusively belongs in the one-flesh relationship of a husband and his wife.[5]

In terms of our orientation to money, it is subversive to admit that greed is not a sign of healthy career ambition but evidence of idolatry. It is subversive to reject our culture's story of the good life, which includes increasing levels of material comfort alongside mounting credit card debt and stinginess. It is subversive to give money away— money which might have been spent on self-serving niceties like vacations and Italian leather shoes. The early church, knowing the apostasy that was on the other side of greed, was none too eager to perform necessary exorcisms of the greedy men and women in their congregations, and it was their common purse and their commitment to care for the poor that testified to their greater hope.

In terms of the magic arts, I can't imagine that readers here regularly struggle with the temptation to have their palms read or fortunes told. But what tactics of divining the future do we engage? And how can our willingness to trust God with the outcomes of our lives be in itself a subversive act? I think of the college admissions process in which our oldest daughter is now engaged and how given to anxiety we might easily be for her and with her. Good money might be spent getting suitable tutors and enrolling her in the best SAT preparatory classes, and there would be a certain legitimacy, of course, in our desire to position her positively for her applications. But there is also an anxious divining we might sinfully engage. (Brownies to the college admissions' office?) At what point do we release our tightened grip of control and surrender our future and our children's future into God's sovereign hands?

And then patience: the unwillingness to return evil for evil. When outrage is the hot take, how great an act of subversion to let oneself be wronged!

We don't live kingdom lives—of sexual purity, generosity, trust, and patience—unless we're imbibing the kingdom story. And we're not imbibing the kingdom story unless we're engaging the subversive act of regular reading, meditation, and study of the Scriptures. Maybe our subversion starts not at the polls but with our smartphones as we deliberately disconnect from the distracting noise of social media and daily submit ourselves to being still and knowing that he is God.

The biblical story is subversive not simply because it inspires a countercultural ethic but because it portends the fateful end of every king and kingdom except God's:

> Behold, with the clouds of heaven
>   there came one like a son of man,
> and he came to the Ancient of Days
>   and was presented before him.
> And to him was given dominion
>   and glory and a kingdom,

that all peoples, nations, and languages
    should serve him;
his dominion is an everlasting dominion,
    which shall not pass away,
and his kingdom one
    that shall not be destroyed. (Dan 7:13-14)

Every president, every king, every prime minister has a term limit. Death ends every reign except one. Politics are not the means of establishing God's kingdom, and no president has messianic promise. Paradoxically, the kingdom of God is a seed, a stump: begun small, subjected to suffering, then filling the whole earth with its branches.

When God's people stand, they sing not "Hail to the Chief" but hallelujah.

QUESTIONS *for* REFLECTION
and DISCUSSION

1. How well have you understood God's kingdom as the golden-spun thread throughout Scripture? What does an A-B-C gospel fail to account for?

2. If it's true that God is one who both self-reveals and hides, what impact does that have on faith? How does this knowledge of God's character influence the way we pray and live?

3. Which surprises you more: That God should favor the least or welcome those with much? Why?

4. Consider the kinds of people you regularly keep company with, the kinds of people who fill up the pews of your church on Sunday morning. Do you see the diversity of God's kingdom represented in their faces? And if not, what could you do to broaden your connection to people unlike you?

5. What have been your assumptions about the shape of kingdom lives? When have those assumptions filled you with a drowning sense of guilt or inadequacy?

6. What would it look like for you to live the kingdom paradox of generosity and enjoyment, which Paul describes in 1 Timothy 6? What greater sacrifice and gladness is God inviting you to?

7. Are there sins you need to confess regarding your involvement in politics or your lack thereof? Maybe you've intentionally cut yourself off from people who disagree with you politically. Maybe you've invested too much hope in the outcomes of local and national elections. Maybe you've practiced too much cynicism.

8. What could it look like to set your hopes fully on Jesus the King? What healing might be possible for the divided evangelical church if we began admitting that God's kingdom was not painted in red or blue?

PART THREE

GRACE

Grace is the very thing that baptizes us as the people of God. Paradoxically, we are plunged by God's own strong hand into death by grace. By grace, we die to self-deception and moral self-assuredness; we die to self-reliance and bootstrap religion; we die to self-trust and to the pocked, unreliable hope that we can save ourselves. All the old ways of earning our keep with God have gone.

The waters of grace are the waters of God's abiding benediction, and the mystery is that they are for you and for me—and not just on Sunday when we arrive in seersucker to church.

9

FREE LUNCH

hen our twin sons turned one, we threw a party, admittedly more for us as parents than for them as children. We had survived a bleary-eyed year, and that survival merited celebration. There was good food. There was shared sweet relief. Then another twin mom at the party dismally pronounced that the hardest year of parenting twins was not the first but the second, "after they learned to walk."

She might have been right. With the exception of the twins' third birthday, when our regular babysitter baked and decorated two cakes in the shape of guitars for a small party of close friends, we celebrated the twins' birthday, for years to come, with as much fanfare as our older three children and their cousins could bring. Then, when the twins started school, we began allowing each of them to invite one friend for dinner and a small shared cake. On their ninth birthday, I made crepes and invited a small crowd of boys who ran circles through our house, slamming doors and hiding in closets. When Andrew and Colin turned ten, I felt more was finally owed to them, especially as they'd been recipients, year after year, of regular birthday party invitations. I planned a small party at an indoor trampoline park and made reservations for dinner at a local restaurant.

On Monday morning, I emailed invitations from my desktop computer. Ryan and I would pick up the boys after school, take them first to the party, then to dinner. But hours after the initial invitations were sent, I checked the calendar on my phone only to realize that the Friday night I'd planned the party was the same Friday night of the school basketball game that the twins (and many of the other boys) were expected to be playing in. (At this point I determined to fix the technological glitch that only allowed me to import the athletic calendars onto my phone, not my desktop.)

A small mistake in the cosmic scheme of life—unless, of course, as I tend to believe, every mistake *is* cosmic and evidence of moral failure. I am a perfectionist in recovery, believing falsely (and still too frequently) that I can only be loved for my rightness. I would have to email all these moms to tell them that I'd planned a party without checking the calendar? I composed a second message and sent it with hopes of *grace*.

To be human is to need the wide and generous berth we often call grace. I would need grace for arriving forty-five minutes late to a scheduled lunch with a friend. I would need it when I called my husband to inform him that I had scrunched our rooftop luggage carrier in a city parking garage, a passerby watching (and swearing loudly) as I did. I would need it for much worse sins than carelessness and forgetfulness. I would need grace for jealousy, grace for greed. I would need it on the Friday afternoon I'd braved rush-hour traffic to pick up my huffy teenage daughter from the mall, she complaining that I'd been so late—and me exploding in rage. Despite all my moral showmanship, I am a walking advertisement for mucking it up and needing people to embrace me anyways.

Grace is the shorthand we often use to talk about the forbearance we hope to receive for our shortcomings. And it's not a bad way to use the word. It is, however, inadequate for what the Bible means when it talks about grace. The biblical word *grace* isn't simply about divine bigheartedness, though it does paradoxically affirm that God, in his perfection, has abounding patience for sinners. His name, in fact, is grace: "The LORD, the LORD, a God merciful and gracious, slow to anger, and abounding in steadfast love and faithfulness" (Ex 34:6). Another part of the paradox of grace, as we'll see in the next chapter, is that even a bighearted God, with so much generous pity for human foibles, could seem to ask so much.

▲ ● ■

Grace is the background of the entire biblical narrative. It's presupposed in the Law and the Prophets and the redemptive history that culminates finally and fully in Jesus Christ. Grace is not, as some suppose, the bright idea God had when the nation of Israel failed to keep his law. God didn't scratch his head after the incident of the golden calf and think to himself, **Grace was not God's afterthought; it was his first thought.** *Demanding obedience is never going to work with this people. I'll have to show grace instead.* No, grace was not God's afterthought; it was his first thought.

From the very beginning of the biblical story, God has always shown himself to be a gracious, liberal giver. Although we can be given to think narrowly of the Garden of Eden as a place of God's restriction rather than God's provision ("Don't eat from the tree of the knowledge of good and evil"), the story didn't play that way. Preceding this forbiddance is a grand and glorious invitation: indulge yourselves! "You may surely eat of every tree of the garden!" (Gen 2:16). Grace is the gravity of our God-breathed world. Out of his own surprising goodness, God made a world and invited us to be his honored guests in it. He set the table. He made the meal. And even more surprising, when we abruptly left that table to heed another dinner invitation, he cleaned up the mess.

God is not just a giver; he's also a forgiver. His grace is a persistent and pursuing one. "God does not wait for Adam to start looking for him; it is God who comes looking with the question, 'Adam, where are you?'—the first words spoken to fallen humanity."[1] One scholar has said that God's grace, which is to say the good favor he lavishes upon the undeserving, can be summed up as simply as this: "God loves because he loves."[2] In other words, God has not chosen to love the lovable and the lovely. Rather, God's love is surprisingly indiscriminate, his favor roving and resting upon those who seem least deserving of it. God's grace is evidenced in his patient pursuit of the mucking-it-up.

> God's love is surprisingly indiscriminate, his favor roving and resting upon those who seem least deserving of it.

God made the nature of his grace plain when he chose Israel as his people. Don't think you're all that, he warned them as they prepared to receive his good gifts of home. You are my treasured people—but not because of any excellency of your own.

> It was not because you were more in number than any other
> people that the LORD set his love on you and chose you, for
> you were the fewest of all peoples, but it is because the LORD
> loves you and is keeping the oath that he swore to your fa-
> thers, that the LORD has brought you out with a mighty hand
> and redeemed you from the house of slavery, from the hand
> of Pharaoh king of Egypt. Know therefore that the LORD
> your God is God, the faithful God who keeps covenant and
> steadfast love. (Deut 7:7-9)

God did not love Israel because it showed a lot of military or moral
promise. Israel was not a recipient of grace because it was good but
because God was.

If grace were like academic standing—vulnerable to loss
whenever you failed to work hard enough to secure it—Israel
would never have made the dean's list. God's people were constantly falling into corruption, doubting God, and chasing after
other gods. They aren't three days beyond the Red Sea, its banks
littered with dead Egyptian soldiers, before they're grumbling
against the leader God has given to them. Three months later,
when Moses disappears into the cloud on Mount Sinai, staying
away for forty days, God's people have given their leader up for
dead. They say to Aaron, "Up, make us gods who shall go before us.
As for this Moses, the man who brought us up out of the land of
Egypt, we do not know what has become of him" (Ex 32:1).

When Moses descends from the mountain, God's holy law in both
hands, he finds that the Israelites, under Aaron's direction, have thrown
an idolatrous party and worshiped the golden calf. He's furious—and
rightfully so. The stone tablets are smashed along with the golden calf,

which is ground into powder and scattered in the water. The people of Israel are forced to drink their treachery. God's angry too. But while he visits a plague upon his wayward people, he doesn't destroy them completely. Instead, his sentence evidences leniency: I'll give you the land which I've promised to your ancestors. I simply won't go with you.

At the site of Israel's unholy revelry, grace is already at work. Nonetheless, it's set to bloom into greater fullness. Moses intercedes on behalf of the people, petitioning God on the basis of his own grace. "How shall it be known that I have found favor in your sight, I and your people? Is it not in your going with us, so that we are distinct, I and your people, from every other people on the face of the earth?" (Ex 33:16). Your grace has brought us this far, Moses argues. Are you really going to withdraw it now? And if you did refuse your grace, could we really be your people without it? Grace is the unmerited favor of God—and paradoxically, Moses seems to think God's people are entitled to it.

Grace is the very thing that baptizes us as the people of God. Hapless sinners, we are plunged by God's own strong hand into death by grace. By grace, we die to self-deception and moral self-assuredness; we die to self-reliance and bootstrap religion; we die to self-trust and to the pocked, unreliable hope that we can save ourselves. All the old ways of earning our keep with God have gone. The waters of grace are the waters of God's abiding benediction, and the mystery is that they are for you and for me, and not just on Sunday when we arrive in seersucker to church. The grace of God opens wide its arms on the very worst of Monday mornings, when the toast burns and there's nothing to pack for lunch, and the car won't start and you aren't given to placidity and prayer but boiling rage. Grace is the best kind of news.

When Moses asked to see the glory of God, God granted him something greater: a glimpse of his grace. I'll let my goodness pass in front of you. I'll tell you my name. Moses, enveloped in the cloud that was God's presence, heard the good news of the gospel that sustains us on those kinds of Monday mornings:

> The LORD, the LORD, a God merciful and gracious, slow to anger, and abounding in steadfast love and faithfulness, keeping steadfast love for thousands, forgiving iniquity and transgression and sin, but who will by no means clear the guilty, visiting the iniquity of the fathers on the children and the children's children, to the third and the fourth generation. (Ex 34:6-7)

God, being righteous, would deal with the egregious affront of human sin—but somehow, in his wrath, he would find a way marked by patience and forgiveness. That is the paradoxical way of grace.

In the cloud that day on Mount Sinai, Moses heard intimations of the cross.

▲ ● ■

We can't, of course, talk about God's grace without talking about the occasion of its fullest, grandest expression: the cross of Jesus Christ. To speak about grace apart from the cross would be like talking about Picasso in terms of his early realist works. In his adulthood, Picasso moved away from realism. When we speak of the greatest achievements of Picasso's career, we don't mention *Science and Charity*, painted however impressively in 1897 when Picasso was fifteen. We talk about his cubist works like *A Girl Before a Mirror*, painted in 1932. Similarly, Moses' experience of

God's grace was a mere foreshadowing when compared to the coming glory of God made flesh—from whose fullness we have all received "grace upon grace" (Jn 1:16).

As Fleming Rutledge explores in her dense book *The Crucifixion*, the cross can't be reduced exclusively to the idea of substitutionary atonement, where God sacrificed himself in the place of guilty humanity. "The Passover lamb, the goat driven into the wilderness, the ransom, the substitute, the victor on the field of battle, the representative man—each and all of these and more have their place, and the cross is diminished if any one of these is omitted."[3] For my purposes here, I can't treat all of these Old Testament themes except to highlight that the cross is where God—the just, the righteously angry, the rightfully wrathful—turns his face away from Jesus that he may by grace behold us. "God, in the person of his sinless Son, put himself voluntarily and deliberately into the condition of greatest accursedness—on our behalf and in our place. This mind-crunching paradox lies at the heart of the Christian message."[4]

To define grace apart from the cross would be to say that God is simply given to leniency. It would be to essentially say that there are rules which we break and break badly, but God reassures us kindly that "It's no big deal." That kind of leniency is what I needed from the mothers to whom I sent the birthday party invitations, but it is not what I have from God. The cross speaks a thundering word about the cosmic big deal that is sin. The surprise of the cross isn't just its leniency but also its violence. It is not I that am strung up for failure but God himself. For all the mistakes and moral failings of humanity, he is the one betrayed and beaten. He is the one crucified and pierced. It is his breath, not mine, that expires—his body, not mine, that is entombed. We deserve his ignominy and get his innocence instead.

How can such grace be?

Christ and him crucified: this is the gospel of grace, the good news that despite our inability to ever make things right with God, he stretches out his hands, east to west, and pays for the forgiveness that can cast our sins into his bottomless ocean of love. The apostles gloried in the cross of Jesus Christ, which should speak of its utter surprise. In the Roman Empire of the first century, a cross was a shame, not a glory. A crucifixion was not something to celebrate but despise.

> Think how loyalty would burn to right this wrong, to clear his memory, to save his reputation, to prove that gross outrage had been done him, to magnify the life so that the death might be forgotten. . . . But nothing of the kind seems to have occurred to the Evangelists. They literally glory in the Cross. . . . They are clear, with an absolute conviction, that the best and most wonderful thing he ever did was . . . to die a felon's death, between two robbers. It was their hero's greatest heroism that he was executed as a common criminal.[5]

We preach God's foolish, heroic grace by preaching the cross.

But if only to believe grace to be true, to believe that God could be this good. Another paradox is this, that while grace is the news we most long to hear, it's one of the hardest things to grasp in life with God. It's hard to receive God's proverbial offer of free lunch in the form of grace. Eugene Peterson, author of *The Message*, concluded this after his tenure in ministry:

> In fifty years of being a pastor, my most difficult assignment continues to be the task of developing a sense about the people

I serve of the soul-transforming implications of grace—a comprehensive, foundational reorientation from living anxiously by my wits and muscle to living effortlessly in the world of God's active presence. The prevailing North American culture . . . is . . . a context of persistent denial of grace.[6]

To receive grace, we need humility. The only prerequisite for grace is empty hands. We have done nothing to make God notice us, and he is not impressed by us. I am not yet brave enough to pray for daily humiliations, as one writer does—but I do pray for humility, if even at the cost which A.W. Tozer describes.[7] "We must invite the cross to do its deadly work within us. We must bring our self-sins to the cross for judgment. We must prepare ourselves for an ordeal of suffering in some measure like that through which our Savior passed when He suffered under Pontius Pilate."[8] We must, in other words, lay down every effort to assuage our guilty conscience, every maneuver to wash and present ourselves clean, and come bathe in the fountain filled liberally with blood.

> Another paradox is this, that while grace is the news we most long to hear, it's one of the hardest things to grasp in life with God.

It is, indeed, a baptism of grace.

10

THE GRACIOUS COURSE
OF RIGHTNESS

*M*olly sat in front of me in American History our junior year of high school. Freshly reborn, I was eager to share my new faith, which I did with Molly. We were friendly in class, and in the spring, I invited her to attend my church's revival services with me and my family. She agreed to come. At the end of every sermon brimming with apocalyptic urgency, the visiting preacher issued his altar call: only a few steps forward and sinners could fall into the arms of Christ. But despite my fervent praying, Molly never walked the aisle, never grasped the preacher's hand to confess Christ. I wonder now, years later, about those seeds planted in history class and in the upholstered pews of Dublin Baptist Church. Since we've reconnected on Facebook, I have learned of Molly's story of recovery. I still want her to find God.

At sixteen, as a new Christian, I understood that courageous witness was one of the terms of this new life. I was saved and others were lost. The gospel of grace was no secret to be hidden under a bushel, even if it meant jeopardizing the popularity I'd been working to accrue since middle school. In the fall of my senior year,

I shook with fear when the words I'd written, as a candidate for a student office, were posted in the student commons. I had publicly called myself a Christian and might as well have been Perpetua in the arena, wittingly lending my body, if not to wild beasts and gladiators, then to the jeering crowds of my peers.

There was a fair bit of legalism in my church tradition growing up, which may have accounted for some of my sobriety and seriousness postconversion. But it wasn't only legalism that bound me to a new way of living after I became a Christian: to bold witness, to sexual purity, to honesty with my parents. I think grace was operative on the old Eve—a grace that surely preceded the transformation but nonetheless obliged it. I hadn't gone looking for God; he'd come looking for me. But when I stepped out to follow, I was set on a new path somehow, leaving behind old ways of being, taking up new ways of moving through this world of resurrection. It was, of course, a very fitful kind of change, and it still is. I wonder about the slowness of my transformation, lagging as I still do behind my own exacting ideals. It's with great befuddlement that I daily receive the surprise of grace: God's patience is wider and higher and deeper than mine.

Though we might think it antithetical to grace, *repent* is the first word of the gospel. This word is not hostile to grace, because grace allows us, poor and beggarly, to hear the call of repentance and enter the broad and spacious places of the kingdom. Grace is the subtle force turning our hearts from the distant country back home. Grace appears, at first, to a hungry person like the simple suggestion of a good home-cooked meal, but when we find it, it turns out to be a much more lavish feast than that. (And then to discover that we are the guest of honor at the Father's table!)

When that younger brother of Jesus' famous parable returned home, only to be picked up indiscreetly by his father and twirled in jubilant, tearful celebration, it's impossible to imagine that he plotted a way to leave again. Where would he go after he'd been welcomed and loved so liberally by this aged man with tears running down his beard? Why would he ever again betray the grace of his prodigal father and return to eating with pigs? He would forever be a debtor to grace. But by contrast, this younger son's older brother had never known grace. He'd never presumed to be a son, only an employee. He had never imagined receiving gifts, only wages, and even these were insufficient for what he took to be the deserved earnings of his hard labor. "Look, these many years I have served you, and I never disobeyed your command, yet you never gave me a young goat!" It's a tale of two sons: one baptized in grace and one refusing its waters.

We don't get grace because we change our lives—but our lives are indelibly changed because we get grace.

▲ ● ■

At fifteen, Brandi Carlile, Grammy-award-winning singer and songwriter, was wearing a swimsuit under her clothes on what was meant to be the day of her baptism. Friends and family had gathered in the small church to witness her submersion into grace. But Carlile's pastor, whom she refers to as "Pastor Tim," abruptly announced that day that he could not and would not baptize her. "He couldn't do it because I was gay, and because I wouldn't say that I was going to change that or that I could change that."[1]

> We don't get grace because we change our lives—but our lives are indelibly changed because we get grace.

During her interview on NPR days prior to the release of her new album, *By the Way, I Forgive You*, Carlile admitted that she'd traveled the "ugly" and "radical" road of forgiving Pastor Tim. She explained that "he called me for days and days afterwards begging for my forgiveness. He said that he struggled with it for so long that he just ran out of time, that he thought he was going to do it right up until the time, but he just couldn't. It took me a long time to forgive him and it threatened my faith; it threatened my self-worth." Her story, broadcast nationally, was meant to illustrate another failure of grace.

There is too much left out of this story to allow me to draw unequivocal conclusions, but I do think it's a story to force an important question: what does baptism into grace mean? It seems, of course, that according to the gospel, anyone can be a candidate for baptism. God has the widest arms of welcome, and the emphatically good news is "that Christ Jesus came into the world to save sinners of whom I am the foremost." If the thief on the cross could be assured eternal blessedness, who's to be excluded from grace?

And yet, though grace will take us as we are, it will not leave us there. Baptism cannot mean that we get to enter and exit the waters the same person. Grace can't mean that we assent to the theoretical idea of God's liberal love but submit to no real transformation. There can be no clinging to death and decay while simultaneously brandishing resurrection. Everyone plunged into the waters of grace emerges with the wrinkly, pink skin of a newly born child of God.

Grace is free, but as Dietrich Bonhoeffer would so clearly define in *The Cost of Discipleship*, paradoxically it is not cheap. "Cheap grace is the preaching of forgiveness without requiring repentance, baptism without church discipline, Communion without confession, absolution without personal confession. Cheap grace is grace without discipleship, grace without the cross, grace without Jesus Christ, living and incarnate."[2] Although Dallas Willard asks an important question in *The Divine Conspiracy* (Can we make grace more expensive?), there is a rightful alarm we sound when grace is being abused, used as cover for flagrant, easy, everyday rebellion— when we'd have the gifts of God without having God himself. "What shall we say then? Are we to continue in sin that grace may abound? By no means! How can we who died to sin still live in it?" (Rom 6:1-2). The curse of the law is that we cannot keep it. The evidence of grace is that we should want to.

▲ ● ■

Grace is utterly transformative: it is the yeast working the dough of the old Adam and the old Eve. To expect transformation is not to negate grace but to affirm its intent and power. This is surely how the early church, in the first centuries after Jesus' death, understood the paradoxical nature of gospel grace.

As mentioned earlier, the compelling witness of the early church was in the changed lives of the Christians. It was for this reason that the church only very hesitantly allowed strangers to explore Christianity and pledge themselves to Christ. While today the only condition for baptism might be whether the baptismal font or pool is filled, in the early church the process preceding baptism sometimes took three or more years. As Alan Kreider details in *The Patient Ferment of the Early Church*, according to *Apostolic Tradition* those wishing to convert to Christianity were "scrutinized" in four important stages, pastors exercising far more caution than Pastor Tim in baptizing new converts.

The "First Scrutiny," as it was called, involved a weekday meeting between the person interested in faith, their Christian friend, and the local Christian teacher. It was not a meeting scheduled for Sunday because non-Christians were excluded from Christian worship services. At this first midweek meeting, Christians were asked to speak on the behalf of their non-Christian friends, specifically on the area of their teachability. "The teachers, with the candidate standing by, pressed the sponsor about the candidate's behavior in light of the church's deep rejection of idolatry, adultery and killing."[3] If the candidate was an actor in pagan theatrical performances, if he was a gladiator, or if she was a prostitute, assurances were needed that these candidates would leave their lines of professional work, which would inevitably make it difficult for them to "hear the word" of Christ.

Having passed the first scrutiny, candidates entered the second stage: the catechumenate. Here they learned not just the teachings of Christ and the master narrative of the Bible but the practices of Christians, such as making the sign of the cross, caring for the poor, prayer, and participation in Christian community. As if in a kind of inverse order, they put on the "habits" of Christians before publicly professing Christian faith. "Refined learning was not the point; the catechesis was not designed to produce sophisticated thought but 'character' and 'virtuous living.'"[4] At the end of this "rigorous" and "unhurried" process, sponsors were again asked to bear witness about the candidates. Did their character reflect the virtues and practices of the church? If the answer was yes, the candidates passed to the third scrutiny, which was preparation for baptism itself.

During these important weeks preceding their baptism and admittance into the church, candidates delved deeper into the essential doctrine of Christian faith; they were prayed over and "exorcised" according to the common tradition of the earlier church. This period, or Third Scrutiny, was set aside for cleansing and for consecration, and candidates needed to "name what they had turned away from as [well as] to name what they turned toward." If any were found not to be living rightly, they were refused baptism. But for those candidates approved by their bishop, they fasted the day before their baptism and kept vigil until the cock crowed on Sunday morning.

As the fourth and final stage, these candidates were baptized naked in a nearby body of water, having stripped themselves naked as if to symbolize that they were "divested of the distinguishing marks on which the hierarchy of ancient society depended."[5] Their nakedness symbolized their embrace of grace. Before being baptized three times—in the name of the Father and of the Son and of the Holy Spirit—these men and women renounced Satan, received the oil of exorcism, and answered three creedal questions. After emerging from the water as recognized Christians, they joined the congregation for worship and took their first Eucharist meal.

▲ ● ■

I'm not sure how many potential Christians would submit to the rigors of such a process today—or how many churches would demand it. We might easily interpret such an approach as overly moralistic and legalistic, a process valuing external behavior rather than inward transformation. Where's grace in all that scrutiny?

The Globe and Mail recently reported on a quickly growing "hipster" church in Toronto's West End.[6] The article opens with the story of Aimee Burke, who found C3 through a client at her salon. Burke attended a service and "felt less empty." "Everyone was within about 10 years of my age and I was 24 years old at the time. They were talking about God, but they looked like people I could party with." Jonathan Li, another C3 attender, describes the welcoming culture of the church: "The big thing here is people come and they don't feel pressured to be anything other than who they are."

In the article, Sam Picken, the thirty-three-year-old pastor of Toronto's newest megachurch, explains his unwillingness to use language that would suggest any kind of judgment. "We're trying not to offer rules, but relationship." The reporter for the piece noticed Picken's disinclination to address incendiary issues such as sexual ethics. "Sexuality is such a personal thing that to make a blanket statement about it feels really objective and impersonal," Picken said. "I see my role not to tell people what's right or wrong or what to do, but to point them to having a relationship with Jesus."

I find Picken's answer wanting. Greater clarity is needed when we are asked to talk about the relationship between grace (which is to say "relationship") and obedience (which is to say "rules"). Paradoxically, grace is not merited by obedience to God's commands, but it obliges us to them nonetheless. God has pledged to purify a people for himself. He is the loving, diligent husband devoted to present his bride without spot or wrinkle:

> What does God say in the Mosaic revelation? He says, essentially, and repeatedly, "I am the Lord who has redeemed you. *And you, my chosen people, shall be like me!*" It is not primarily a case of "because I have redeemed you, you *must* be like me." Again and again simple indicative statements are made which promise that Israel shall be a people holy to

Yahweh. . . . You *shall not* have any other God or idols, etc. . . . You *shall* honour your parents, you *shall not* be murderers, idolaters, thieves, liars, coveters. This is not the vain wish of a god who is hoping for the best, but doubts whether he can really accomplish anything much; it is the promise of a future reality. . . . The people of this holy God shall be holy![7]

There is fruitful tension between grace and law, law and grace, and paying attention to that tension helps us avoid the *either* of legalism (which separates God's law from grace) and the *or* of antinomianism (which separates God's grace from obedience). It is a paradox that God's gratuitous grace should rain on the righteous and the unrighteous—*and* that obedience should be demanded for no other apparent reason than "it *is* his word."[8]

"Law is not the source of rightness," wrote Dallas Willard in *The Divine Conspiracy*, "but it is forever the course of rightness."[9] Perhaps those might have been words that Pastor Tim could have spoken to Brandi Carlile, encouraging her by God's grace to live a holy life of celibacy. Perhaps these are words that Picken can speak to his congregation when discussing sexual ethics. The Bible is not silent on these important contemporary questions, and it calls us not into oppressive restriction but to broader places of abundant life. It's worth saying that in the name of freedom and autonomy, it's the devil who comes to steal, kill, and destroy.

As Jesus has told us, we must be careful to be too carelessly plunged into the waters of grace: "Whoever does not bear his own cross and come after me cannot be my disciple. For which of you, desiring to build a tower, does not first sit down and count the cost, whether he has enough to complete it?" (Lk 14:27-28). We are not saved by effort, but neither are we saved from it. By grace, God will have his way with us, "to will and to work for his good pleasure" (Phil 2:13).

Every good work of grace God begins, he completes.

11

BIRDS AND
BROKEN WINGS

*Y*up . . . yup . . . yup. Now release the wheel. Good. A little bit of gas. Yup."

This is a transcription of our oldest daughter's first driving lesson with me the summer before her junior year. Her younger sister video recorded it from the backseat. Although I had tried telling Ryan that it was his responsibility to teach our oldest to drive, I was the unfortunate one with flexibility in my summer schedule. But I am happy to say that on her first day on the road, I was uncharacteristically calm and encouraging as Audrey jerked to stops and starts in a nearby neighborhood, which I had specifically chosen for its wider, quieter streets.

I did not scream. I was not given to hysterics. My instructions were as clear as I was clearheaded. Were Camille's video submitted to a court of law, a judge might find me an exemplar of patience. But given the opportunity, my children might approach the judge's bench on that day of examination and submit other evidence to set the public record straight. They would tell stories of my fault-finding, my exaggerated demands, my intolerance and inflexibility, my daily failures at grace. They would sardonically point out that not everyone appreciated the gift of criticism as much as I did. They would recount stories of their own witness of paradox—when I had angrily punished them for their sin of unrestrained anger.

I fear that my own children have been victims of my wild swinging between what I have wrongly considered to be the poles of grace and truth. One day, I am full of liberality, choosing to ignore the unmade beds, the forgotten lunchboxes, the shoes kicked off at the front door and left for me to trip over. On these sunny days, I choose silence as a way of choosing grace, figuring that God surely works in the lives of his children apart from their nagging mothers. When my cup of proverbial grace runs over, I swallow another high-pitched moral lesson; I distract rather than discipline; I choose to see childishness rather than sin. When grace of this cheerful sort reigns, I am easy-tempered and easily forgiving, and the mood in our home is breezy.

Then, unexpectedly, the weather changes. It's as if the liberality of my "grace" runs dry, and my anger burns hot like the sun. I am punctilious and exacting. I neglect no error. I bang my hand against the table, telling my children that they're the worst kind of house-mates, inconsiderate and lazy for failing to clear their dinner dishes. I rain truth like sulfur and fire rained on Sodom and Gomorrah—and watch, with horror, when they are, one by one, mercilessly licked up in the flames. Surely there are truths I must say, and surely this is not the way to be saying them.

Who will teach me the real meaning of grace?

▲ ● ■

The difficult task of loving God's people and saying hard things to them was given to the prophets of Israel. Return to the Lord, they said time and again, calling out Israel's sins in as unapologetic terms as "whoredom." Return to the Lord, and he will return to you! The prophets pronounced God's impending judgment for the northern and southern kingdoms, not because they relished, like Jesus' disciples James and John, the thought of God sending consuming fire to lick up his enemies; rather, their calls of repentance were, paradoxically, calls of blessing.

Every hard word spoken by the prophets was a gracious invitation to turn from sin and flourish under God's good rule. They recalled the pronouncements heralded from the summits of Mount Ebal and Mount Gerizim when God's people were poised to enter the promised land: "Cursed be anyone who does not confirm the words of this law by doing them" (Deut 27:26); "All these blessings shall come upon you and overtake you, if you obey the voice of the LORD your God" (Deut 28:2). Even Jonah knew the sobering grace behind every hard word of God: "O LORD, is not this what I said when I was yet in my country? That is why I made haste to flee to Tarshish; for I knew that you are a gracious God and merciful, slow to anger and abounding in steadfast love, and relenting from disaster" (Jon 4:2). It was God's infuriating grace that set Jonah to flight.

The hard words of the prophets weren't, of course, always received as expressions of grace. When the prophets of God stood to proclaim war and famine, drought and plague, they often incited fury and persecution. People plugged their ears, dismissing their gloom and doom in favor of the sunshine-and-rainbows sermons, which the false prophets preached. "Ah, Lord GOD, behold the prophets say [to the people], 'You shall not see the sword, nor shall you have famine, but I will give you assured peace in this place'" (Jer 14:13). *Peace* was an easier word to say, an easier word to hear. And *peace* was also a false and tickling word which could not save God's people. This *peace* was no expression of grace.

Amos, the sheep breeder and vinedresser, was plucked from the fields to speak God's hard words and was met with characteristic resistance from Amaziah, the priest of Bethel. Amos, this outsider from Judah, had dared forecast destruction for the northern kingdom in a time of that nation's great prosperity and geopolitical security. In Amos 7, it is recorded that Amos saw three ominous visions: a plague, a devastating fire, and a plumb line by which Israel is found wanting. Amaziah runs off to report to the king, Jeroboam II, that Amos has conspired against him, speaking these words of overthrow:

> Jeroboam shall die by the sword,
>   and Israel must go into exile
>   away from his land. (Amos 7:11)

"The land is not able to bear all his words," Amaziah tells Jeroboam before attempting to send Amos away. Go back to Judah. Don't prophesy your hard words here. But Amos reprises the same theme of God's pending judgment in even more vivid terms:

> Your wife shall be a prostitute in the city,
>   and your sons and your daughters shall fall by the sword,
>   and your land shall be divided up with a measuring line;
> you yourself shall die in an unclean land,
>   and Israel shall surely go into exile away from its land. (v. 17)

Rather than taking Amos's hard words as evidence of a spiteful spirit, we must recall the sight of him in the very beginning of chapter 7. When God pronounces judgment, Amos falls pleading to his knees:

> O Lord God, please forgive!
> How can Jacob stand?
> He is so small! (v. 2)

Amos was a man of great courage—and also great pity. In preaching hard words of repentance, he had the hopefulness that characterized all God's faithful prophets: "Who knows whether he will not turn and relent, and leave a blessing behind him?" (Joel 2:14).

To speak God's hard words well requires this of us: a deep, visceral compassion for the people for whom hard words are necessary. We can't revel in hard words, can't feel smugly satisfied in the task of speaking them. We certainly never see arrogant contempt in the ministry of Jesus, who spoke a lot of hard words. When he spoke the hard words to the rich young ruler entangled by his love of money, Mark tells us that Jesus, "looking at him, loved him" (Mk 10:21). Jesus' hard words for this man were not the alternative to love; they were the evidence of it. "Go, sell all you have and give to the poor, . . . and come, follow me." This was a hard word for a man who'd padded his life with comfort, but seen another way it was a word of total freedom and greater joy: the man was promised greater treasure. Even the hard words Jesus spoke to the religious leaders were words of love. Whitewashed tombs, he called them. But such willingness to call a pharisaical spade a spade must have been great relief to the people bound by the Pharisees' excessive burdens of religious duty.

We follow in the footsteps of this Jesus, who came with great love and hard words, this incarnate Son of God "full of grace and truth" (Jn 1:14). And as those on whom the Spirit of Jesus is now poured, ours is now the prophetic task: "Would that all the LORD's people were prophets, that the LORD would put his Spirit on them!" (Num 11:29).

▲ ● ■

Paradoxically, grace doesn't dispense with hard words, even if it never lets us say them harshly. Unfortunately, most of us have fallen prey to a person all too happy to speak a hard word. I was in my late twenties when I was crushed by someone's hard words. Admittedly, I had been wrong about something, and I had tried saying sorry. (She wasn't, however, returning my phone calls.) After a month had passed and she did finally agree to meet with me, I thought we'd work to reconcile our relationship. She, on the other hand, seized it as an opportunity to remind me not simply of the wrong I'd done but the *wrong I was*. My personality was unlikeable, she said. I was belligerent, defensive, and selfish; the most recent incident was only one of many to support her accusations. I sat listening in stunned silence, then drove home in blinding tears. It was a conversation never to forget—and never to stop hurting.

By God's amazing grace, there were things to be learned from those hard words spoken so many years ago, and whatever her real intentions in speaking them, those words helped me grow in greater understanding of myself. As God mysteriously does, he wrought good from pain. But I don't hold up her example for imitation. Whenever we speak hard words, grace would beg we speak them with great carefulness, continuing to believe and hope the best about the person receiving them. As Scripture reminds us, our anger doesn't do God's work well.

I was reminded of this reading Leslie Leyland Field's *Forgiving Our Fathers and Mothers* several years ago. Fields's childhood was difficult. She suffered poverty and hunger; there were the cruel indifference of her father and the abuse he'd inflicted on her sister. Rightfully, she had so much resentment toward her father, but she also understood that she must somehow forgive him. Fields began discovering that forgiveness required compassion, much like the compassion the good Samaritan had shown to the beaten traveler. Often, those who've wounded us have themselves been wounded, and it is our task to "discover and remember [their] frailty."[1]

"None of this is about excusing sin," Fields clarified. "Don't patronize [those who've hurt you] by relieving them of responsibility. If they are merely excused, there is no opportunity for them to acknowledge their responsibility, to repent, to seek forgiveness, to move away from the habits and wrongs of the past to another kind of living and relating to people."[2] Forgiveness doesn't dispense with hard words, but it does dispense with the demand for recompense. To forgive, in Old Testament terms, is an act of Jubilee. We forgive our debtors—as we, of course, have been forgiven.

A hard word can be a means of grace. When we rightly identify a wrong we have suffered, when we take up the courage to tell the difficult truth, the injuring party is invited to pursue more life-giving ways in the relationship. Hard words seek to heal, not to rend. Similarly, for those of us tasked with shepherding others, whether children or congregants, when we speak hard words of necessary repentance to those in our care, we are inviting them to leave death behind and take up life instead.

That's what Eliza Spurgeon believed as she raised the son who would become the great nineteenth-century English preacher. Charles Spurgeon remembered his own rebellious heart as a young boy. "As long as ever I could, I rebelled, and revolted, and struggled against God. When He would have me pray, I would not pray, and when He would have me listen to the sound of the ministry, I would not. And when I heard, and the tear rolled down my cheek, I wiped it away and defied Him to melt my soul." But Eliza persisted to teach the Scriptures to her defiant son as to all her children, never hesitating to ask her children about their spiritual state.

Most searing in Charles's memory was the sound of his mother praying for each of her children: "Now, Lord, if my children go on in their sins, it will not be from ignorance that they perish, and my soul must bear swift witness against them on the day of judgment if they lay not hold of Christ." Many years later, Charles would recall that prayer: "How can I ever forget her tearful eye when she warned me to escape from the wrath to come?"[3]

As parents and as pastors know, we can speak hard words to no apparent avail. We can believe the best, and people can keep choosing the apparent worst. Our hard words are no guarantee of repairing a relationship or reconciling someone to God. The sight of their struggle is like the sight of the fledgling bluebird that has tumbled out of her nest. Jonas McAnn, the fictional pastor writing letters to his small-town congregation, describes such a scene:

> [The momma bird] couldn't return her chick to safety. She could only circle near, watch with care, and offer the best she had to give, no matter how meager. So she stayed close and hoped favor would bend their way. I think this is how it is for

most of us who love someone or carry concern for this world. We will never be able to right all wrongs or heal every wound. We cannot keep harm from those dearest to us. To love is to do our best and then to hope, to have faith. Often, love means simply circling and staying near—trusting that this will somehow prove enough.[4]

That's the most vivid picture I've had to date about grace as we hold it out to another person. It's hopeful work, and it's hard work. Oh, I wish that my hard words could heal every pair of broken wings. But they can't, of course: not even the wings of my own children.

Still, I keep trusting that grace will prove enough—both for them and for me.

12

THE EFFORTS
OF GRACE

We gathered in my living room on a wintry Sunday evening, several of us warming our backs to the fireplace. Our small group discussion turned toward the spiritual disciplines. Sarah, seated sideways on the sofa, began to confess the constant knot of anxiety she carried in her chest. "I think God's calling me to be still," she confessed. "And he's been saying this for months. But I just can't." She described lurching from bed every morning in dull panic, imagining urgencies and the consequences of failing them. "I can't even be still for five minutes," she admitted.

By God's grace, daily stillness has not usually been a difficult discipline for me. Excepting the season that I nursed the twins, ever since high school, I've kept quiet mornings with God. Now that I'm in my forties, I'm waking up even earlier than I used to, meeting with God at five a.m. when the house is shrouded in dark and swaddled in silence. It's my one still hour to know that he is God. If the rest of the day is thrown to the dogs, as it almost inevitably will be, the next day rises with the mercies of another morning.

I may meet God fairly easily in the morning, but there are disciplines which feel as difficult to me as stillness does to Sarah. Fasting, for example. I wasn't raised in a tradition where fasting, as a spiritual discipline, was emphasized, although in college, keen from reading Richard Foster's *Celebration of Discipline*, I began to regularly fast, disappearing from the cafeteria and into a small student chapel on campus every week. God met me hungry. But after I graduated, I fasted only intermittently. In fact, the last food fast in recent memory wasn't all that recent. It was Lent 2007. Jevonte, then fourteen months old, returned to our care for the second time after his mother had placed him in temporary custody with the ministry of Safe Families. Jevonte had come to us the first time when he was only ten months old, and he had been an especially demanding baby, suffering from lack of routine and consistent nurture. When he returned, several months later, he arrived as headstrong as ever in an especially full season for our family.

Before Jevonte's arrival, I had committed to giving up dessert for Lent. After his arrival—and several days of his relentless crying, I reneged. It was not the time to be giving up on a little comfort.

I don't want to admit that I turn to food for comfort. That I do, however, has been made apparent from the most recent fast I engaged following my conversation with friends around the fire, which turned on Matthew 11:28-30: "Come to me, all who labor and are heavy laden, and I will give you rest. Take my yoke upon you, and learn from me, for I am gentle and lowly in heart, and you will find rest for your souls. For my yoke is easy, and my burden is light." Together, we had mused about the paradox of spiritual transformation, that though the way of Christ is a way of grace, it is also a way of the yoke. There were constraints to be fitted around ourselves, constraints against which we would inevitably chafe.

It had been many months that the still, small voice had tried making his persistent way with me regarding some of my unhealthy patterns of eating. I had tried confessing those patterns to God. I had said sorry. I had promised to do better. I wasn't guilty of binging on gallons of ice cream, maybe, but I did reward long hours of work with small indulgences. I finished the Nutella. I snuck furtive spoonfuls of ice cream. I fished M&M's from the trail mix. There were times I considered engaging a fast as a way of breaking my slavery to a series of afternoon treats, but the idea was always quickly abandoned. It was easier to tell myself that this wasn't really a sin problem, that I could quit anytime. I continued living the law of exceptions, forgetting how quickly exceptions become rules. We are made slaves more easily than we think.

I needed a bodily practice for a disordered, bodily appetite. I needed a spiritual discipline for greater physical freedom. I needed grace, and paradoxically, it was going to take some work.

▲ ● ■

On the day that I stood by the lake, at fifteen, to hear the voice of Jesus, it wasn't as if we had an appointment. Grace came to me unbidden, which is why I call it grace. And this is the consistent testimony of grace in the Scriptures—that it arrives like an expensive package we haven't ordered. We don't lift a finger to take hold of saving grace, only stand under its rain shower with open mouths, trying to gulp down its goodness. We receive grace and then keep on receiving it, never graduating from the generosity of God. Grace is the way we begin, and grace is the way we continue.

Grace is the forever good news that there is always more to rely on than our own efforts and energies, which flag and falter and fail.

But to say all of this might seem to suggest that human passivity is the stuff of grace—that we are an inert receptacle and God, giver and gift. Truthfully, in terms of the grace that rescues us from our lostness and blindness and death, I am given to describing it exactly like that. (I am a Presbyterian after all.) But in terms of the grace that resurrects us to new life in Christ, I want to fumble for better words, words that convey our responsibility in God's project. Human agency is not sufficient for justification, but human agency is critical for sanctification. And this is just a fancy way of saying that we must *work* in a life saved by grace.

The only kind of faith that the Bible mentions is obedient faith (Rom 1:5). Faith isn't a rote rehearsal of the Nicene Creed; it produces a changed life. And a changed life is neither an accidental outcome nor a haphazard endeavor. Ancient church father Tertullian put it this way: "Christians are made, not born."[1] On the other side of saving grace, we are meant to put ourselves, by whatever means possible, in the path of transformation. And this is what the spiritual disciplines are: not the rain shower of God's grace but the effort to get outside.

The late Dallas Willard wrote brilliantly about spiritual formation as it paradoxically depends on both grace and effort. When he described the process of discipleship that we each must undertake, he says unequivocally, "This is an active, not passive, process, one that requires our clearheaded and relentless participation. It will not be done for us."[2] This is to clear up a great misunderstanding about grace. Grace does work we cannot do, but it does not relieve us of the responsibility to work. In other words, grace provides all that we need in terms of the tools for growing a life deep in Christ, but it will not spare us the effort of picking them up. "We must stop using the fact that we cannot *earn* grace . . . as an excuse for not energetically seeking to *receive* grace. Having been found by God, we then become seekers of an ever fuller life in him."

"Grace is opposed to earning, but not to effort."

We see this principle demonstrated in Jesus' interaction with the crippled man at the pool of Bethesda. It is rumored that the pool, periodically stirred up by angels, has miraculous healing powers. When the blind, the lame, and the paralyzed lower themselves into the water, they can expect to see and to walk and to dance.

On the day that Jesus walks by the pool, he meets a man who has been an invalid for thirty-eight years. Thirty-eight years this man has spent under those five roofed colonnades, waiting for the beginning of the rest of his life. We might imagine him, years earlier, hopeful and young, a man willing to suffer whatever necessary injury in his crawl toward the waters. But on the day that he meets Jesus, he is remarkably older and noticeably more lethargic. Jesus' first question to him is a strange one: "Do you want to be healed?" (Jn 5:6).

Jesus had never needed to ask blind Bartimaeus if he wanted to see. Jesus had never needed to ask the bleeding woman, after she'd touched his robe, if she wanted to be made well. But here he is asking a man, lying on a mat with a pair of raisin legs, if he wants to walk. The man's answer, of course, reveals why the question needed asking: "Sir, I have no one to put me into the pool when the water is stirred up, and while I am going another steps down before me." What's clear from the passage is not just this man's failure to get into the pool but his unwillingness to take responsibility for that failure.

Eighteenth-century Bible commentator Matthew Henry makes this observation: "The angel stirred the water, but left the diseased themselves to get in." This man wanted grace to stir the pool—and grace to do his walking. But Jesus would not abide that kind of soul paralysis: "Get up, take up your bed, and walk. *And at once the man was healed*" (Jn 5:8-9).

I am imperfectly describing the mechanics of grace: in truth, grace stirs the waters, and grace gets us into the pool. But this isn't against our effort or even apart from it. We must make a response to grace, and it's this response, writes A. W. Tozer, that makes a saint of an ordinary man or woman.

> Pick at random a score of great saints whose lives and testimonies are widely known. . . . I venture to suggest that the one vital quality which they had in common was spiritual receptivity. Something in them was open to heaven, something which urged them Godward. Without attempting anything like a profound analysis, I shall say simply that they had spiritual awareness and . . . they went out to cultivate it until it became the biggest thing in their lives. They differed from the average person in that when they felt the inward longing they *did something about it*. They acquired the lifelong habit of spiritual response.[3]

Spiritual response, said Jesus, is an easy yoke and a light burden, which is to say something lightweight and yet something to be carried nonetheless. Perhaps we could think of the work of the

Levites during the forty years of wilderness wandering. By God's initiative of grace, he had declared his intent to dwell in the midst of his people, giving them instructions for building his "house."

Worship is always God's gracious invitation to his people. But to really imagine the tabernacle, though, is to acknowledge the laborious work required for transporting this mobile house of worship. The cloud would stop, the Israelites would camp, and the Levites would be tasked with arranging all the furniture of God's house according to specification. Then three days or three months or three years later, the cloud would lift, the Israelites would pack bags, and the Levites would be left to dismantle the crossbars and frames, the goatskin coverings, the embroidered curtains, the altar, the table of incense, the lampstand, the ark. While the rest of the Israelites had backpacks and roller bags, the Levites had heavy trunks to carry—and the trembling fear of doing it right. The tabernacle was, in a metaphorical way, the Levite's easy yoke and light burden.

We too have things to carry even if we have no trembling fear. *Do you want to be healed?* The gospel invites us to "with confidence draw near to the throne of grace, that we may receive mercy and find grace to help in time of need" (Heb 4:16). The pool has indeed been stirred by Christ, and with his gracious help, we will walk toward it.

▲ ● ■

Writing in the mid-twentieth century, A. W. Tozer lamented the difficulty of helping people to form the habit of spiritual response in a machine age. Spiritual response is, by necessity, a patient and unhurried effort. "A generation of Christians reared among push buttons and automatic machines is impatient of slower and less direct methods of reaching their goals."[4] How might it be possible to help people long for God and linger with him?

The challenge, more than fifty years later, seems even greater. We are ever more conformed to habits of speed, ever more impatient with the prospect of delay. Our media-saturated lives are noisy and distracted, and it's only with intentional effort that we can quiet the clamor to hear God. I see that people want methods easier and sexier than Tozer proposed, but I'm not sure they can be improved upon. In fact, his advice bears striking resemblance to the counsel of the early church: turn to God, exercise yourself unto godliness, and seek to develop the powers of spiritual receptivity by trust, obedience, and humility.[5]

Here is the sole effort we must make: we must give grace as much access to our lives as possible. First, in some quiet pocket of our day, let's immerse ourselves in the true and surprising story of God. Let's wear out the bindings of our Bibles, irreverently spill coffee on their pages, and ask God to drive his words straight through the bone and marrow of our thinking and intending and desiring. Let's turn to God with all the prayerful hope that his grace is sufficient to meet us in our wondering and wandering. With God's help, let's then put on new habits of being: honesty, sexual purity, generosity, courage, patience. Let's take up the ancient disciplines of solitude and silence, prayer and fasting, worship and study, fellowship and confession, never thinking that God's business is information but transformation. As there is failure, let us confess; as there is renewed intention, let us seek accountability and help. (We're damned to think that a godly life is a solitary one.) Let's join the great company of sinners and saints in a local congregation and commit together to put one foot in front of another every day for the glory of God.

God is a speaking God—and we are meant to be his responsive people. All of it is grace.

> **Here is the sole effort we must make: we must give grace as much access to our lives as possible.**

"Oh that my ways may be steadfast in keeping your statutes!" While Psalm 119 extols the excellencies of God's Word, it does not extol the excellencies of human effort. The psalmist does actively seek God, but this is not to say that he relies on his own seeking. Rather, he seems to understand that no matter how zealously he seeks, more will be required than his zeal. "Incline my heart to your testimonies," he petitions. Transform my desires, in other words. Then he confesses, "I have gone astray like a lost sheep; seek your servant."

God seeks his servants. That's the paradox of grace behind all our seeking.

QUESTIONS *for* REFLECTION
and DISCUSSION

1. What are ways that you resist grace? Maybe you find it hard to forgive others, harder still to forgive yourself. How do you try earning God's favor rather than simply receiving his gratuitous offer of free lunch?

2. How does grace—this idea of God's indiscriminate and patient love—inspire you with hopefulness for others, even for yourself? And how is grace different from simple leniency?

3. Read the psalmist's words from Psalm 119:159: "Consider how I love your precepts! Give me life according to your steadfast love." How convinced are you that obedience is the path to your "best life now"?

4. When are you subtly persuaded that God's rules are narrow and repressive? What particular temptation would lose its allure if you began believing that your greatest freedom was to be found in faithfulness to God?

5. Describe a time when someone spoke hard words to you. Did you experience it as an act of grace? Why or why not?

6. Is God calling you now to speak hard, gracious words to another person? What would it look like to exercise compassion in that speaking?

7. In your spiritual life, how is God calling you to stretch your legs and get into the pool? What fears hold you back? What temptations?

8. What habits of spiritual response can you cultivate in your daily life as a way of making yourself more receptive to God's grace? How will you make yourself accountable to forming these habits?

PART

FOUR

LAMENT

The impolitic plea, or *lament*, is an ancient prayer tradition in the Bible. In language that seems hardly admissible in God's throne room, as men and women pray to God, they try making faithful sense of the mystery of their suffering and the love of God in the worst of circumstances. Lament, with its clear-eyed appraisal of suffering alongside its commitment to finding audience with God, is a paradoxical practice of faith.

13

FLUENCY IN
THE LOUD GROAN

*T*he steel specter of the bridge grows in the distance. I draw a bath of muted anxiety, wondering if the guard rails are tall enough to break our falling. We cross the bridge. I tighten my grip. This is the gesture of interposing my will between one involuntary jerk of the wheel and a pendulous future.

When the highway puts down her feet again, I wonder about this fear of bridges. Rationally, I tell myself that it is entirely normal to have grown less comfortable with the wide-open spaces of highways and the habits of perilous speed. For more than six years, we've lived in the city of Toronto, and my daily shuttling kids to school requires skillful maneuvering around the congestion of local traffic and distracted pedestrians. I may not be able to cross a bridge without panic, but I can parallel park my car.

I want it to be this. I want this fear of bridges to be a sign of skill gone rusty. But I fear it is more ominous. I fear it is aged, full-bodied grief. Because though I am forty-three and my father and brother have been dead for more than twenty years, the specter of the bridge pends every possible rupture, every possible falling and

breaking in this fragile life. Two decades later, I am finally reconciling myself to a world of constant, unavoidable loss.

When I was younger, life neater, I used to think of death as an
event. People put sweaty palms into your hands, squeezed your
shoulders reassuringly, whispered banalities in your ear on their
way to paying respects. I have stood in that line and received those
murmured sympathies. At eighteen, at twenty-three, I thought
death was something to be buried, to be moved past, to be retrieved
only as a dusty relic from memory's attic. Twenty years ago, I was
naive enough to think that new life could be made in the absence
of death, as if death and all its griefs ever fully absented themselves.
Now that I am older, death feels no longer like an event.

It is the dangling proposition at every bridge.

"This isn't Disneyland," writes Sallie Tisdale in her published
book of essays, *Violation*, which gropes in the darkness for answers
to human suffering. The collection spans thirty years and explores
a broad range of topics: flies, elephants, moray eels; abortion, che-
motherapy; family relationships, technology, the writing life. As a
Buddhist (and professional nurse), Tisdale defends the obligation
to embrace death and dissolution rather than resist it. To a fair
degree, she manages the dispassion and "emotional equanimity"
called Buddhist virtue.

But there are also moments that Tisdale can't help herself, oc-
casions when she is caught begging for answers: "At times there is
a loud voice inside me, complaining indignantly: *Explain this!*
Someone please explain this."[1]

Without the overwrought effect of emotional tirade, Tisdale
exposes how life has been more than occasionally cruel: a father's
alcoholism and abuse ("the debris of many whiskey-laden years")[2];

a mother's distance and neglect; the growing gulf between siblings; betrayal at having raised children only to lose them, first to
rebellion, then to growing up. "I hadn't expected to be knocked to
my knees in grief when he marches out after I tell him to stay,"
Tisdale writes in "Scars," which chronologically sketches her eventually troubled relationship with her son at four, eight, fifteen, and
finally nineteen.[3] Tisdale even (or especially) insists that moth-
erhood belies the intractable mercilessness of life that she un-
earthed as a child after she and her brother had buried the carcass
of a turtle, hoping to later reclaim its shell. Weeks passed, and they
discovered that most of the shell had disappeared. "The earth was
more fierce than I had guessed."[4] With delicacy and restraint,
Tisdale masterfully touches the quick of human vulnerability: "It
is so ... dangerous to love somebody."[5]

Nine years ago, I was pregnant with my twin sons when I called
my mother from Walmart. "What was that brand of hand lotion
you were telling me about?" But our cellular connection suffered,
and as she told the story later, my voice broke intermittently,
making it sound as if I were gasping for air.

The proposal of death.

My childhood asthma, which I had long outgrown, had returned
during this last pregnancy, causing fierce and uncontrollable fits of
coughing. I had spent more than one night at the local emergency
room, even Christmas Eve three weeks before the twins' early arrival. With a greater need for oxygen, I was breathing with ever
greater difficulty.

"Can you breathe, Jen?"

"Of course, Mom. I'm fine. I just want to know about the lotion."

The words scrambled. Intimations of falling, falling, falling.

"Jen, are you okay?"

The gasping sounds continued. My mother imagined my body deflating like a balloon.

"Call 9-1-1!"

"They came and turned him into juice and soil, the Buddha flowing gloriously like cream into the ground," Tisdale writes in her essay, "The Sutra of Maggots and Blowflies."[6] Death, according to Tisdale, demands equanimity, and she rehearses acceptance, however much she also secretly demands explanation for the falling. *Explain this!* She knows how we indulge indignant complaint against the fierceness and fragility of the earth, however unoriginal this begging for our lives, which arrives sounding like the tired obscenities of Tisdale's "Gentleman Caller."

"Dirty jokes and pleas for God are all the same," she writes. "All he can do is pick up the phone and make his impolitic plea."[7]

▲ ● ■

The impolitic plea, or *lament*, is an ancient prayer tradition in the Bible. In language that seems hardly admissible in God's throne room, as men and women pray to God, they try making faithful sense of the mystery of their suffering—and the love of God in the worst of circumstances. Lament, with its clear-eyed appraisal of suffering alongside its commitment to finding audience with God, is a paradoxical practice of faith. In the book of Psalms, we see suffering of all kinds: enemies, threats of death, false accusation, betrayal. Further, we see suffering of these external varieties causing internal anguish: lost appetite, constant crying, insomnia. Most generically, the psalmist might refer to his suffering as the "trouble" he's in, a word that provides broad connection to the hardships of modern life: divorce, financial insecurity, disease, job dissatisfaction, unemployment, prodigal children, crises of identity. "In the day of my trouble I seek the Lord" (Ps 77:2).

Trouble can be minor, of course: a slight inconvenience or unexpected bother. Road construction. A long line. A banking error. It was trouble, no doubt, which caused the rudeness of the patron in the grocery store when I'd unwittingly cut in front of him. But the worst kind of trouble—the kind of trouble that inspires lament—is the chronic kind, which time does not ease but inflames. No doubt it was trouble behind the recent phone call of a friend, asking if I knew about the heartbreaking arrival of divorce papers. His three years of separation have ended abruptly in a letter arriving by certified mail. The trouble continues.

The Bible is full of trouble. Reading Scripture, I have the opposite reaction of a friend who complains, in our weekly Bible study, about the Bible's penchant for happy-clappy endings. (She and her husband have struggled with infertility, and we were discussing the ending of the book of Ruth.) Although I know the biblical narrative ultimately ends happily, I can't help seeing a vast amount of trouble in this book that preaches good news: trouble for Adam and Eve and trouble for their sons, trouble for Lot and trouble for his wife, trouble for Abraham and trouble for Sarah, life-altering troubles for Jacob, who believes his favored son to be dead. "No, I shall go down to Sheol to my son, mourning" (Gen 37:35). Having only begun with Genesis, it's impossible to deny the inordinate amounts of trouble the saints face.

What could surprise someone unfamiliar with the Bible is how much space is devoted not just to trouble but to the complaint, anger, and doubt of God's people in response. Implausibly,

paradoxically, conversation with God about trouble can be ruth-
lessly honest, even deliberately uncheerful. We call that conversation *lament*. Lament is "howling prayer," according to Dan
Allender and Tremper Longman.[8] Lament is praying in a "minor
key," writes J. Todd Billings.[9] As Ellen Davis, professor at Duke
Divinity School, explains, the psalms of lament seem to violate
all the rules we assume must govern our conversations with God.
When God's people suffer and speak to him about it in Scripture,
they often become self-focused, impolite, vengeful even, refusing
to evade or excuse, gloss or gussy up.

Suffering, with its power to shatter, makes something brittle of
pretense, and lament broods over God's silence, God's absence,
God's seeming indifference in trouble. Can we really pray like this?
Is not the holy, holy, holy God offended by the brutality of our
impious conclusions?

O Lord, how long shall I cry for help,
    and you will not hear?
Or cry to you "Violence!"
    and you will not save?
Why do you make me see iniquity,
    and why do you idly look at wrong? (Hab 1:2-4)

But for all its seemingly impolitic, impious qualities, lament is a
confession of faith. Maybe mustard seed faith, maybe angry faith,
but faith nonetheless. It is not an abandonment or denial of God,
but an affirmation of his reality, even his goodness and power. It
might shock us to learn that in the book that is purportedly a collection of praises, there are more psalms of lament than psalms of
thanksgiving and praise. In other words, most psalms are not tame

and tepid; instead, they read like nasty letters to the editor. "O my God, I cry by day, but you do not answer, and by night, but I find no rest" (Ps 22:2). In the psalms of lament, people ring God on the day of trouble and demand an accounting for his inaction. This is complaint, to be sure—but it is also the persistence of faith that hounds God until he answers.

Our human impulse—as spectators to trouble, not sufferers—is, of course, to defend God from accusation. This is the tact of Job's friends when trouble visits him in the form of marauding armies, howling winds, and loathsome sores. They need an answer for Job's trouble, and the only answer they can provide, which protects the reputation of God, is Job's hidden moral failures.

> **For all its seemingly impolitic, impious qualities, lament is a confession of faith.**

Behold, blessed is the one whom God reproves;
> therefore despise not the discipline of the Almighty.
For he wounds, but he binds up;
> he shatters, but his hands heal. (Job 5:17-18)

You only have trouble, Job, because you have rightfully deserved it, his friends tell him. This is logic as doctrine, certainty instead of mystery. But their play at piety ultimately grieves and angers God, who asks Job to offer sacrifices on their behalf. Job has raised an impolitic plea and learned, only at the end, that God commends him for speaking rightly. "My servant Job shall pray for you, for I will accept his prayer not to deal with you according to your folly. For you have not spoken of me what is right, as my servant Job has" (Job 42:8). For the little we can conclude from the book of Job, we know at least this much: lament is vindicated.

Yet even though Job faithfully and rightfully laments, he doesn't get the answers he demands. And while he eventually gets more children, he doesn't get back the sons and daughters he lost, their bodies broken by the collapsing walls of the house struck by storm. This is the example I cite in Bible study with my friend, who is angered by Ruth's happily-ever-after. We could say that Job's story ends happily; we could also say that his suffering has a residual quality to it.

I can't help but see that certain forms of suffering are indelible in this life, especially the suffering of the grave. As seems true with Job, mystery can bring us to modest faith, but modest faith cannot bring back the dead. Sometimes there is no untangling the why. "The focal point of the book is not God's justice at all, but rather the problem of human pain: how Job endures it, cries out of it, wrestles furiously with God in the midst of it, and ultimately transcends his pain—or better, is transformed through it."[10] As Ellen Davis remarks, "Job gives us immeasurably more than a theology of *suffering*. It gives us the theology of the *sufferer*." She continues, "The one who complains to God, pleads with God, rails at God, does not let God off the hook for a minute— she is at least admitted to mystery."[11]

In other words, it can be the paradox of the impolitic plea—this unholy wondering in the midst of suffering— that brings us face-to-face with God.

▲ ● ■

I almost lost seven-year-old Camille on a Toronto subway platform. When I had turned, from inside the train, to see my daughter—outside, standing alone—my feet became bricks of indecision. The doors chimed and began closing. A stranger jumped to pry them open, and I pulled her inside, smothering her small body to my chest. She didn't even know our phone number.[12]

Six years later, Camille, almost thirteen, was the happy new owner of a cell phone. It was Sunday morning, and I was riding the subway with her to church, rehearsing the route she would take home alone. "You're going to have to look for the stairs that say 'Northbound' on the way back," I said, reassuring myself that her older brother and sister had come of age in exactly this same way.

The train rumbled in as we stood several feet behind the thickly painted yellow line that portended the sheer drop onto the tracks. As I always did standing behind that line, I imagined the accident, the surprise violence that sent us, unprepared, over its edge.

We boarded a near empty car. Several stops later, a large man boarded, muttering under his breath. The doors closed, and when he shuffled past, I saw and heard him in vague outline—thick parka, wool hat, noisy feet. His wily, unpredictable body brushed past, and I pulled Camille's girl-ness—pencil frame and prairie chest—against me. She watched out the window, resting her head on my shoulder. Warily, I watched him.

He set a coffee at his feet, pulling a muffin from a paper bag and smearing it with cream cheese. He tipped his head back, licked the knife. He turned it over and licked again, worrying it like a bone. I watched him, suddenly remembering the day that we had been a gaggle of bosoming high school girls, unapologetically loud and conspicuously American in the bowels of the Paris subway. Though we had been warned about pickpockets, we hadn't noticed him approaching from behind. After he had put his hand up my friend's skirt, we were too stunned to take record of his disappearing face.

That had been the first time I knew the subway as arousal and drunken breath, violence and vulnerability. It was the first time I'd learned to be afraid.

The city bobbed in and out of view. We swayed silently with the train. Then the man suddenly howled. Camille startled upright. It was a wounded sound: a lament, guttural and anguished. He lurched to his feet, began pacing the car. I pulled Camille closer. We braced for another outburst, clutching our bags tightly against us and casting our eyes to the floor. I ticked the remaining minutes of our ride.

That's when I saw it: the muddy river of coffee running under his seat, toward the front of the train, its tributaries, sweet and creamy, filling the car with the smell of accident. On the one hand, it was the mishap of one ordinary morning, the crisis of one inadvertent kick of the foot. On the other, it was a sign of betrayal—this world's crushing inhospitality. If the man's sob of grief could have seemed utterly disproportionate, I found it exactly right.

Isn't this the cruelty of suffering: not just that it's hard and heavy but that it's always so extemporaneous? In a church scene from Terrence Malick's film *The Tree of Life*, Father Haynes stands to deliver a sermon from the book of Job: "Job imagined that he might build his nest on high—that the integrity of his behavior would protect him against misfortune. And his friends thought, mistakenly, that the Lord could have punished him because secretly he'd done something wrong. But, no, misfortune befalls the good as well. We can't protect ourselves against it. . . . We vanish as a cloud. We wither as the autumn grass, and like a tree are rooted up." Father Haynes continues, "Is there some fraud in the scheme of the universe? Is there nothing which is deathless? Nothing which does not pass away?"

When the bridge looms into view, I am thinking of this fraudulent universe, wondering how we, as people of faith, abide in hope when we are not deathless. Death is trouble of the most longstanding kind. And what lament teaches me, at the very least, is that it is not equanimity that I need in the face of death but outrage. Because in some very real way, we have been cheated by death, dealt the worst of hands by our cursed mortality. Death is a thief, and it must be reckoned with.

As Ellen Davis has paradoxically written, "The prayer in which we most need fluency is the loud groan."

14

COMPLAINTS
DEPARTMENT

*T*he school receptionist distributed an evasive announcement of my brother's death to the staff mailboxes. "Jen Michel's brother, David, died suddenly on October 12." I imagine her fingers poised over the keyboard, puzzling over what details to include of his suicide. She left room for speculation—as I would, for many years to follow when people asked, "Do you have any siblings?" I learned to answer vaguely: "It's just me." Sometimes, if the mood struck, I answered more honestly. "My brother died, but it's a long, painful story." However I answered, I always tried strangling too much curiosity. It was easiest to bury mention of the dead.

On my first day back to teaching after my brother's funeral, I avoided the front office and those mailboxes stuffed with condolences. I wanted to be left alone, left to the business of getting on with it, which is what I did when the students filed into my class that day. "Thanks for your concern. I was with my mother this week in Ohio." Even my rowdy eighth-period sophomores fell into the tacit agreement that no more questions would be asked.

They finished their work. I stayed dry-eyed. How valiant it can feel, at least in the moment, to put death under your feet.

Routine was, in those days, a welcome boundary to grief. In the months following my brother's death, I got dressed in the morning. I left the apartment. I graded essays, attended faculty meetings. But in the late afternoon, when I returned from school after a long day of teaching and coaching, that neatly bounded grief spilled its edges, descending and drowning as a throbbing, blinding headache. For months, I would dim the lights in our apartment and crawl into bed, suffering the heat of grief with a cold washcloth over my eyes. Only my husband, Ryan, knew how death had put me under its heavy feet.

My father had died just four years earlier when I was in my freshman year of college, and I was supposed to be practiced in this thing called loss. His death had been sudden, stealing him away without time for goodbye. I took a week to grieve the loss before returning to campus and cloistering myself in the basement of the library. I earned my best grades that semester, as if to prove that you need not be a victim when death comes for someone close to you. You too can wear heavy boots. But at the time of my brother's death, I was an amateur all over again, not having the least idea how to simultaneously live and carry death with me.

We don't get good at grief. Suffering is inventive. I suppose that's why I still devour books on the subject. Because even though my father and brother have diminished to mere specks in the rearview mirror, even though life today idles along with relative peace, I feel the need of death's know-how.

I don't want it taking me by surprise again.

"I'm falling asleep," were the last words Sheryl Sandberg, COO of Facebook, spoke to her husband, Dave Goldberg. They'd been

sitting beside a pool somewhere in Mexico where they were
spending the weekend celebrating a friend's birthday. Dave excused
himself to go to the gym before dinner, and Sheryl dozed, returning to their room without Dave, thinking nothing of his pro-
longed absence. She showered, got ready for dinner, but when she
arrived in the hotel lobby and noticed that Dave was not among
their friends gathering for dinner, fear surged in her chest. She and
a couple of friends ran to the hotel gym where they found Dave
collapsed beside a treadmill, lying in a pool of his own blood. He
was dead on arrival to the hospital.

In her book *Option B*, coauthored with Wharton psychology
professor and friend Adam Grant, Sheryl talks about the journey
back from death to life and how she navigated the turbulent waters
of bereavement with her two young children. For months, she de-
spaired that life would ever return to anything resembling the state
of "normal." She worried that her children, having lost a father so
young, would always acutely and irreparably suffer his loss. But
Adam Grant's research on resilience provided a kind of cerebral
anchor at the time, giving her the empirical data on how people
overcome trauma and develop resilience.

Sandberg began learning to avoid the pitfalls of personalization
("This was my fault"), pervasiveness ("This ruins everything"), and
permanence ("I'll never be happy again"). The woman who had
barreled her way to professional success in Silicon Valley was now
admirably putting the force of that indomitable will toward putting
death under her feet.

"It's okay to feel what you feel," was one of the grief rules she
posted above where her children's backpacks hung in their home.
Sheryl also told her daughter and son other things like it's okay

to be jealous of friends who have fathers; it's okay to tell people that you don't want to talk about it. Sandberg gave herself and her children permission to let grief unravel at will, however undignified the unspooling might be. The assumption in all of this was that it was

> Lament isn't the road back to normal. It's the road back to faith.

better to *feel* than to numb, better to *rage* than repress. Grief permitted the casting aside of courtesies and formalities.

There is a lot of wisdom in Sandberg's approach. But it isn't to be confused with biblical lament. For while biblical lament is honest and honesty important, the act of complaining to God is not primarily about venting our emotions, not primarily about building endurance, not primarily about clawing our way back to happiness.

Lament isn't the road back to normal. It's the road back to faith.

▲ ● ■

"My voice to God—let me cry out. My voice to God—and hearken to me." Robert Alter's translation of Psalm 77:1 rings with an insistence lost in the more muted translation of the ESV: "I cry aloud to God, aloud to God, and he will hear me." In Alter's translation, what leads out of the gate of prayer is the raging bull of *his voice*. As if dispensing with the formalities of salutation and address, the speaker is confident in one thing: the shrill ferocity of his own complaint. There's a sense in which the confidence, at the very opening of the psalm, is not in God—or his goodness or power—but in the speaker's own set of lungs. Despairing of God (as the psalms of lament do, at least in the beginning), the speaker puts his bets on his competence at raising a stink.

This is the paradox of lament as we have it in Scripture: not just complaint, not just complaint *about* God, but complaint *to* God!

Lament is not just emotional tirade, not just the soul-bearing so-
liloquy of forgottenness and forsakenness. It is a frantic plea di-
rected heavenward: "My God, my God, why have you forsaken me?"
(Ps 22:1). At its core, biblical lament is always articulated as prayer.

Lament is the prayer of people who suffer, and it follows the
impulse of prayer that John Calvin saw modeled in the psalms—
prayer in which nothing is concealed. Lament is a practice for reckoning with our pain and reckoning with the God who has not
eased the difficulty or grief. But it makes us more than whiners; it
makes us whiny pray-ers. Lament comes to us as the invitation to
name our complaints to God; it gives us the mysterious latitude to
exercise faith as small as the mustard seed of outrage. When the
only courage we have is the courage to complain, then we pray that!

Ellen Davis notes that the medieval church made much greater
use of the book of Job, full as it is of lament, than we do presently.
She also points out that the Episcopal Church, in its Burial Office,
has discreetly excised the impolitic conclusion that Job draws at the
opening of his drama of terror: "The LORD has taken away" (Job
1:21). "Have we grown afraid to lodge the responsibility for our grief
with the Lord, as Job so consistently does?"[1] In other words, there
seems to be a modern apprehension about bringing complaint to
God. Maybe we fear bruising God with our honesty. Maybe we fear
having to endure greater suffering as discipline for our cheekiness.
Maybe our acquisitive lifestyles are distractions we use to numb the
suffering that would ultimately be worthy of lament.

It's certainly true that few of us are learning the language of
lament on Sunday mornings, where chirpy faith seems preferred to
guttural sorrow. "Our own worship is deformed by our failure to
bring the language of suffering into the sanctuary as an integral

part of our weekly liturgy," writes J. Todd Billings, author of *Rejoicing in Lament*. Most fundamentally, maybe we're just not sure that lament is part of the *faith* experience. Maybe it belongs more rightly to the shadowy realms of doubt.

But as Davis concludes, in the pattern of lament that we see in the Bible, complaining to God is an act of faith precisely because "when you lament in good faith, opening yourself to God honestly and fully—no matter what you have to say—then you are beginning to clear the way for praise."[2] With only two notable exceptions in Scripture (Psalm 39 and Psalm 88), the needle of biblical lament doesn't get stuck in the groove of despair. Lament voices complaint, but it advances toward confidence; it names petition, but then marches toward praise.[3] In fact, this is the arc we could trace over the entire book of Psalms, which ends with five rousing anthems of praise. Lament will have no final word.

This isn't to say that the movement of lament is always linear, of course. In Psalm 22, we see the back-and-forth motion of lament. Two steps forward toward trust—

> You are holy,
> enthroned on the praises of Israel.
> In you our fathers trusted. (vv. 3-4)
> You are he who took me from the womb;
> you made me trust you at my mother's breasts. (v. 9)

Then three steps back toward anguish:

> But I am a worm and not a man,
> scorned by mankind and despised by the people. (v. 6)
> I am poured out like water,
> and all my bones are out of joint. (v. 14)

Lament has the clumsy, unsteady motion of a toddler learning to walk; he's moving toward his mother with her arms outstretched, and yet there are sure to be spills along the way.

As aforementioned, twice in the book of Psalms there is no resolution to the discordant lines of lament. Psalm 39 begs God to look away from him, ending with this terrible finality: "Mere breath all humankind" (v. 13, Alter's translation). In Psalm 88, the speaker suffers the terrors of God without relief: "Why, LORD, do You abandon my life, do You hide your face from me?" He casts about for help and finds none. "My friends—utter darkness."[4] Even despondency has made its way into the book of Praises.

▲ ● ■

There is a great deal of polite praying in church. I am guilty of it myself. We are pious and solicitous with God. In public practice at least (and I reckon also in private), prayer seems to be a lot of saying what we think God wants to hear. We play the notes of prayer, but there's no real music—which is to say, the communion with God that is intended to be as intimate as sexual love. Prayer is meant for undressing us, for making it possible for us to know and be known by God. Pretense in prayer is a lot like kissing with your clothes on.

Before sin entered the world (and with it, shame) humanity walked naked and unashamed with God, and in our radiant purity there was nothing to hide. In a very important way, lament cries out over the wreckage made of God's very good world post-Genesis 3. It says, "This has not always been, and it should not always be!" And in a kind of redemptive irony, it's the very act of complaint that returns us to our prelapsarian state of candor, if not to our former innocence. Lament won't settle for hiding in the trees when God must be found.

Hear my prayer, O Lᴏʀᴅ,
and give ear to my cry;
hold not your peace at my tears! (Ps 39:12)

The psalmist, like Job, wants an audience with God. He wants God to act the role not of impassible judge but of compassionate father. See my tears, and let them move you to action! What can often feel so difficult about many types of suffering is the way that they render us powerless. When the doctor delivers the terminal diagnosis, when a child wanders far from faith, when a husband betrays the vows of marriage, we are left to reel at our impotence. These are not situations we can grab by the scruff of the neck and shake into compliance. No, they are bullies, attempting to make cowards of us.

Suffering does not obey our ultimatums, but lament reclaims some of our agency. "Laments are refusals to settle for the way things are. They are acts of relentless hope that believes no situation falls outside Yahweh's capacity for transformation. No situation falls outside of Yahweh's responsibility."[5] There is pluck to lament, pluck to its faith. Lest we think that faith is slack surrender to God's will, the testimony that we have in Scripture is of faith paradoxically emboldened to ask, to question, to challenge, to complain.

And just to clarify, this asking, this questioning, this challenging, this complaining are practices of *faith* because they rest on the very nature of who God is. In other words, it's the steadfast love of the Lord that endures forever which makes sense of complaint, which grants it audience. If the world is ordered according to randomness, then complaint has no rightful place. And if God is neither good nor powerful, then we are better off handling our miseries on our own. But if God is sovereign, if God keeps his

promises, if God is a rescuer, then lament seems suitable to the
world he inhabits and presides over.

In Psalm 77 the psalmist opens with the tearful weariness of
lament. He is not sleeping, and the spiritual practices which
once brought God near seem now only to illuminate the divine
absence. "When I remember God, I moan; when I meditate, my
spirit faints" (v. 3). He tries calling forth the stories of the "days
of old," as if to will himself to remember who God is and what
he has done.

> Will the Lord spurn forever,
> and never again be favorable?
> Has his steadfast love forever ceased?
> Are his promises at an end for all time?
> Has God forgotten to be gracious?
> Has he in anger shut up his compassion? (vv. 7-9)

He asks these questions precisely because he and the people of
Israel have not always known God to be a flight risk in the day of
trouble. No, there had been their miraculous rescue from Egypt,
when God had plucked them from the hands of their enemies and
delivered them to safety. A wall of water had stood in the way, but
God had "led [his] people like a flock by the hand of Moses and
Aaron" (v. 20). The exodus had testified to God's unfailing love. "I will
remember the deeds of the LORD;
yes, I will remember your wonders of
old" (v. 11).

Lament is this habit of petulant wondering: has God's mercy dried up, or can it be counted on still? To complain to God is to risk on continuous supply.

Lament is this habit of petulant
wondering: has God's mercy dried

up, or can it be counted on still? To complain to God is to risk on continuous supply.

Several years ago, my husband received an email, along with two other members of the corporation's leadership team, from a disgruntled employee. Without warning, the small gym used by employees had been closed without plans to reopen. This woman was writing to plead for intervention. The email opened with this address: "Dear Big Cheeses." Lament starts exactly this way: an impolitic plea of prayer addressed to the head of the complaints department.

"Dear Big Cheese."

15

UNFINISHED
BUSINESS

*D*o you always let your children ride their bikes in the
street?" Olivia has stopped by to pick up my twin sons
for a playdate with her own son. I try defending myself to my new
friend, a vigilant mother of two young boys. But it isn't long before
the two of us are remembering aloud the story of the little seven-
year-old girl killed a couple of summers ago in our neighborhood.
She left the park where her mother had remained behind with a
younger sibling and crossed the street alone, by the library, to walk
the two blocks home. It was a route they had practiced together,
but a truck rumbled along, and the driver failed to stop. I can't turn
at that stoplight without thinking of brown-eyed Georgia, without
wondering about the persistent grief of her parents, without asking
why their number, of all the available numbers in the world, should
have been picked.

Weeks later, my children aren't carelessly riding in the street but
safely down the manmade peninsula of Toronto's Leslie Street spit.
There are no oncoming cars, just open road extending several miles
into Lake Ontario and bending for spectacular views of the city

skyline. The peninsula ends at a gravel beach of sorts, shored by heavy concrete rubble and filled with the detritus of urban life: bricks, bent rebar, and other construction waste.

It is not safe to walk these beaches, especially barefoot. But Ryan and I let the kids dismount their bikes and scale the mounds of rubble anyway, even pick up pieces to throw into the water. We watch them from behind as they skip rocks across the surface of the wind-chopped water. Colin, the youngest of our twin boys, heaves a large triangular piece of concrete in the lake, and it jumps almost imperceptibly. When he turns to catch my eye, I throw an approving fist in the air. "Casting all your care upon [the Lord]" (1 Pet 5:7 KJV). It's one of the first verses I ever learned as a child, and it's the verse that comes to mind on this windswept day. I imagine those rocks as the bulky burdens of trouble. I see them disappear beneath the surface, skipping until submerged into God's great care.

Lament is the practice of casting *care* on the Lord. And these worries and anxieties, big and small, ordinary and monumental, matter greatly to the God who meticulously accounts for every strand of every person's hair. It is, of course, entirely right and appropriate that we plead for God's intervention in all forms of suffering, no matter their size and shape. Because as every parent knows, it's not the nature of the injury that inspires your concern, but the tears.

> You have kept count of my tossings;
>> put my tears in your bottle.
>> Are they not in your book? (Ps 56:8)

We can't know how full those bottles, how long that book.

There is every indication that God's mercy is as reliable for suffering that is banal as for suffering that is big. And this is one of the great mysteries of divine love, that I need make no defense for the worthiness of my trouble and the rightfulness of my need. "Lord, help!" is the refrain of Psalm 107 in the New Living Translation, which struck me on a day that was troubled in the most inconsequential of ways. I had been feeling reluctant to bring the anxieties of that day to God, but the Scripture issued an unapologetic invitation. Cry out and wait for God's rescue, even if it means nothing more than the lice are gone. (Yes, lice!)

Nevertheless, in its most biblical form, lament isn't only the practice of bearing our personal grief before the Lord. Though we have every reason to bring every burden to God, that isn't the only way we must be praying. Perhaps even more importantly, biblical lament is an expression of our anguish over the wrecked state of the world. It's the way we cry out about the debris of death and disease, of injustice and oppression. We scale the mound and howl with the wind.

"How long, O Lord?"

▲ ● ■

The title for the book of Lamentations in the Septuagint, the Greek translation of the Old Testament, is "Wailings." Its authorship is credited to the prophet Jeremiah, and its occasion is the destruction of Jerusalem. Babylonian boots have trampled through the city of Jerusalem, crushing the material promises of God under its feet. The city of David lies in rubble, its walls broken down, its houses destroyed. Solomon's temple, once a bright beacon of divine blessing, has been burned to the ground, the gold, silver, and bronze carted off, the priests murdered in cold blood. Only a remnant remains in the city to observe the extent of the destruction. Included in their numbers is God's weeping prophet.

All around him Jeremiah sees the destructive force of God's judgment. Because Judah has not returned to the Lord, the Lord has turned against them. With hurricane force he has roared with wrath, leaving devastation in his wake.

> He has laid waste his booth like a garden,
>   laid in ruins his meeting place;
> the LORD has made Zion forget
>   festival and Sabbath,
> and in his fierce indignation has spurned king and priest.
>   (Lam 2:6)

With tragic irony, the noise of Israel's defeat resembles the sound of their former religious celebrations: "[The Babylonians] raised a clamor in the house of the LORD as on the day of festival" (Lam 2:7). In the temple, there's the unholy sound of reveling.

But in his book of wailings, Jeremiah does not survey the destruction only to lament the loss of close friends and immediate family and the destruction of his beloved little bungalow at the end of the cul-de-sac. No, Lamentations is not so much a catalog of Jeremiah's personal sorrow (even if Jeremiah speaks of his own physical, emotional, and spiritual suffering at the opening of chapter 3). Instead, the weeping prophet shares in the nation's grief. "The Lord has trodden as in a winepress the virgin daughter of Judah. *For these things I weep*" (Lam 1:15-16). When Jeremiah wails, he cries out for other people's children, for other men's wives, for other neighbors' houses. His wailings seem to be the holiest anguish of all: those we bear on behalf of another.

It is easier, of course, to act the part of dissatisfied customer—to complain, not about the greater injustices people suffer in this world but the momentary lapses in our own comfort and convenience. I am well-practiced in this. Construction on the new subway line near my house has been limping along for years now. And though I should be grateful that the city of Toronto has not, after years of construction, reversed plans for the project and filled in the excavation sites, as they did in the mid-1990s, I still indulge complaint. I can't leave my neighborhood later than 4 p.m. lest I'm stuck behind an inchworm of cars. And more recently, more road construction has begun on another major artery, and with this new construction, coupled with the subway construction, the fifteen-minute morning drive to our children's school sometimes slows to a crawling thirty-minute commute. I suffer the drive and feel it to be a suffering. But the weeping prophet offers a better lesson: learn to grieve what God grieves.

Just as there is a necessary learning in our life of desire,[1] there is also a necessary learning in our life of grief. Paradoxically, while we feel pain and pleasure to be the most instinctive of emotions,

Learn to grieve what God grieves. we don't instinctively love what God loves, nor do we reflexively grieve what he grieves. We must be apprenticed in God's sorrow. As J. Todd Billings explores in *Rejoicing in Lament*, there are distorted forms of lament, including the complaint "about interruptions in [our] comfortable, middle-class lifestyle, without an eye toward seeking God's kingdom."[2] The troubles we regularly bring to God might be more closely examined for what they reveal about the things we treasure, the things we most vigilantly protect, the things we cannot lose.

If the only troubles we bring to God are those that belong to us, we are not praying in the tradition of God's weeping prophet. As Augustine argued—and as Billings picks up in his own book— Scripture becomes "a divine pedagogy for our affections—God's way of reshaping our desires and perceptions so that [we] learn to lament in the right things and take joy in the right things."[3] All too easily, we can feel our own suffering to be the heaviest. It seems truer to say that God wants us to bear the weight of weeping for another.

Soong-Chan Rah uses the book of Lamentations as the foundational text for his own book, *Prophetic Lament: A Call of Justice in Troubled Times.* The anguished heartbeat of the book is about the failure of lament in the white American church. People of privilege grieve too little, writes Rah. Instead of suffering with our suffering brothers and sisters of color, we have insulated ourselves in separate churches and taken up a happy-clappy songbook—one altogether different from "The Sorrow Songs," which W. E. B. DuBois describes as "the music of an unhappy people, of the children of disappointment; they tell of death and suffering and unvoiced longing toward a truer world, of misty wanderings and hidden ways."[4] Lament is the willingness, at least in one sense, to sing the spirituals left to us by the slave era.

My sister-in-law, a social worker in the Chicago public school system, describes the daily challenges her students of color face. Many of them, sons and daughters of gang members, brave the threat of death in order to come regularly to school. Often, in these embattled cases, school administrators file requests for special assistance in getting a child to school. *Safe passage,* they call it, as if getting to school were as treacherous an endeavor as braving the open ocean in a leaky raft. On the Chicago public schools' website, students can click on maps to find routes of safe passage between home and school. As if to reassure, students are to understand the important partnership existing between local schools and the Chicago Police Department. I notice that none of the top ten academically ranked elementary schools are listed.

I think of how I ready my own children for school: I buy backpacks and lunchboxes, colored pencils and textbooks; I stock the refrigerator and pantry. But in cities like Chicago, parents consult maps for their children's *safe passage*. To arrive safely at Lawndale Elementary School, where my sister-in-law and her family live, the yellow line of safety circles around whatever danger lies north of Douglas Boulevard between St. Louis and Homan Avenues.

It makes me wonder: *Can God's people learn to care about all his children getting to school in the morning? Can we grieve when they don't, as if our own sons and daughters were lost? And wouldn't that be the truest kind of lament?*

▲ ● ■

Lament is an expression of anguish over the suffering we own as well as the suffering we borrow, and it has a way of involving us when we'd rather stand aside. As most of us know, a broken world writes endless invitations, throws parties every day of the week. There is grief enough to go 'round. I used to see obedience as the uncompromising willingness to show up to those parties, to solve those problems, to tirelessly support those broken people. But heroism only lasts so long, and when it's finally paid out, we are left with lament. How long, O Lord?

Lament paradoxically necessitates great faith—and a different kind of participation with God. We come only to lament when we've abandoned our messianic intentions. Only when we see the disaster as too extensive, our capacity as too limited, only when we finally admit our powerlessness are we readied for lament—readied to bring the divine business back to its rightful owner.

It does, of course, require grieving how much of that business is unfinished: in our own transformation, in our relationships, in our neighborhoods, in the world. Lament, as compassion, is the heaviness of care we heave into God's great ocean of love. When will death finally be submerged—and with it, everything that makes the world breakable? When is God going to do something about all this debris?

Seven years after moving from Chicago to Toronto, I still haven't broken myself of the habit of listening to Chicago Public Radio

> **Lament, as compassion, is the heaviness of care we heave into God's great ocean of love.**

whenever I'm at the kitchen sink. (If Chicago's weather calls for rain in the morning, my children will be wearing boots to school.) In the car, however, I try tuning into the events happening right around me: the hiring of a new museum director at the art gallery on Ontario, the opening of a new play at the Fringe Festival, the update on a union strike by teachers at the Toronto District School Board. It's one way of keeping place in Toronto, of learning what it can mean for me to be a better neighbor in my city. On many days, the headlining news also provides the content for lament.

On March 31, 2015, a sex trade worker was abducted at the intersection of Shuter and Sherbourne, just blocks from the commercial building our church owned and occupied at the time. I learned about her abduction and captivity from a radio interview with the man who eventually rescued her. She was held captive for five days in a neighborhood not far from my house, rescued only when this man, walking his dog, heard her pleading for help from a front porch where she had managed to escape. During the radio interview, the man described how he'd found her: wrists and ankles bound with packing tape, naked from the waist down.

His voice catches, and silence unfurls. I am sobbing at the steering wheel.

How long, O Lord? When Jeremiah looked out over Jerusalem, he sobbed at the godforsaken sight of her.

> My eyes will flow without ceasing,
> > without respite,
> until the LORD from heaven
> > looks down and sees;
> my eyes cause me grief
> > at the fate of all the daughters of my city. (Lam 3:49-51)

Lament sees. Lament sobs. Lament cries out to the only one capable of reversing any of our godforsaken fortunes. And though lament could seem like despair, it isn't: because the act of crying out is the act of imagining intervention. It's one way we ask God to deal with his unfinished business.

As D. L. Mayfield describes in her book *Assimilate or Go Home*, Frank Laubach, missionary to the Philippines, had the practice of walking to the top of a hill near his home and willing God's presence and love over his small town. Mayfield, whose work with immigrants brings her often to holy wailings and dead ends, has taken up Laubach's practice on her running route. She stops on a bridge to look over her city and its high-rise apartments. "I stand quietly, eyes focused on the thousand souls that I never could fully see. And I try to be like [Frank], try to pray the love of God on the city. I try to imagine it as an ocean of longing, the beams of the sun transforming into the only presence big enough for all our needs."[5]

Lament brings us to the top of the hill. We see the debris, imagining it cast into the bottomless waters of God's great love. Paradoxically, lament, as holy complaint, is hope for the day when the sun rises.

Never to set.

16

A SUFFERING GOD

I like saying that I brought everything into this marriage. It's certainly true that I owned the standard transmission, two-door red Honda Accord, which I had to teach Ryan to drive. But it's probably truer to admit that Ryan was the one with the $30,000 a year job, a salary we could have hardly imagined before it was offered, while I, on the other hand, had my student teaching practicum and zero income.

Our early years were hardly lean, even if we shopped at the discount grocery store and ate dinners at home. Even in the lean years—if they can be called that—we afforded the luxury of saving. We paid down college debt. I went to graduate school. We saved for the down payment on our first house—a two-bedroom ranch four blocks north of the library in a quiet, safe suburb of Chicago.

When I married Ryan, he was "chief" of nothing. He was a long-haired economics and mathematics major. In the spring before our college graduation, the career development office at Wheaton arranged for two job interviews for Ryan: one as an actuarial student at a local insurance company, one as a consultant. Not wanting to travel after we were newly married, he took the former. And this began the falling into two decades of corporate earnings. Of all the numbers to draw, why was ours chosen for this more-than-enough? It's the burdens of others that weight this relative ease. Several years ago, the Truth and Reconciliation Commission of Canada concluded its six-year mandate to collect the stories of indigenous children who suffered in the nation's residential school system. In the 1870s, church-run residential schools began to receive federal funding for educating aboriginal children. The explicit goal was assimilation. Between the 1870s and the 1990s, more than 150,000 children were taken from their homes, and those children suffered not just the emotional trauma of separation from their families but also documented physical and sexual abuse. It is a story of national shame, and there is a national cry for repentance. After holding seven national events, the TRC decided to award, on average, $20,452 to every living residential school survivor. For those who suffered more severe abuse, additional damages were awarded. With almost thirty thousand claims resolved, the average payment for those awards was $114,179.

The money is paid, and the interview archives are now housed at a national research center at the University of Manitoba, Winnipeg. But the suffering continues. Suicide rates among First Nations people in Canada are, by certain estimates, tens of times what they are in nonaboriginal communities. Chiefs and councils are declaring states of emergency in their communities when their people, at alarming rates and impossibly young ages, choose to die.[1]

I wonder what might have been if I'd been born aboriginal in Attawapiskat. Or even black in Baltimore.

In his book *Between the World and Me*, written as a letter to his young son, Ta-Nehisi Coates describes what it was like to grow up in West Baltimore. "To be black in the Baltimore of my youth was to be naked before the elements of the world, before all the guns, fists, knives, crack, rape, and disease."[2] Coates's memoir is ripe with fear, fear of the police brutality and endemic racism that make his son's body as "breakable" as the body of his college friend, Prince Carmen Jones, who was killed, unarmed, by police.

Coates rejects the faith of his forebears, even the faith of Prince's mother; he doesn't sing the spirituals of the slave era, which lament suffering but also proclaim hope. He grieves injustice, but he cannot join the praying assembly at his friend's funeral. "When the assembled mourners bowed their heads in prayer, I was divided from them because I believed that the void would not answer back."[3] Why bother with complaint, Coates concludes, if there is no one behind the counter to receive it?

There is a way to complain about injustice in the world that has nothing to do with faith. There is a way of hoping to repair the world that is nothing about relying on God (and all about trusting in one's own do-gooding). There is also a way of existing **The way** in the world that doesn't complain or grieve but **of Jesus is** rather insulates itself from the everyday travesties of **the way of** injustice. But there is yet another way, a more Godlike **lament.** orientation to the world, and it's the paradoxical way of weeping. It's the way of Jesus outside the tomb of one of his closest friends, tears falling despite all his reassurances about resurrection and life. That way of Jesus is the way of lament. Lament cries out its anguish to God. It mourns a breakable world and the bodies in it. It survives on the hope of a return call.

A hope that doesn't disappoint. Because God's body broke too.

▲ ● ■

When the psalmists fell into despair over the "trouble" of life, they did not acquiesce to the cruelties of the world; they complained to God. But they didn't just complain as they prayed; they also *remembered*. They rehearsed the stories their mothers and grandmothers and their fathers and grandfathers had told them around the dinner table and at bedtime and on pilgrimage to the temple: stories of plagues and dry ground and bread that fell with the dew.

Lament was carried on these acts of remembering. Whenever it became difficult to see God in the present, these ancient men and women conjured up scenes from the past. They let their history part the clouds of divine obscurity and tell them something about God's nature. They returned, again and again, to God's own self-revelation in the wilderness when Moses heard Yahweh proclaim his own name: "The LORD, the LORD, a God merciful and gracious, slow to anger, and abounding in steadfast love and faithfulness" (Ex 34:6). Faith was not always seeing God in the present tense; it was often the act of observing God in retrospect.

When Christians lament, they also rehearse a story: the story of God's breakable body and the power that put it back together again. That story of death and resurrection belongs in the same book as Israel's stories of exodus and Passover, of tabernacle and temple, of priest and prophet and king. This story of God's broken body is one of continuity and discontinuity, continuation and beginning.[4] It is a story of death, but also a story of God's victory over all that is lamentable. If God's body broke, the resurrection stakes this bold claim: lament will have no last word. Brokenness is a middle act, not the final scene.

When Peter stood at Pentecost to address a bewildered crowd, he insisted to those gathered, *you're telling the wrong story*. These Galilean men whom you have observed speaking in foreign languages are not drunk, Peter corrected. They're filled with the Spirit, whom God promised, through the prophet Joel, to send. This Spirit has been poured out on the offering of God's breakable body, which is now raised up and exalted. Today, we greet the day of the Lord, Peter proclaimed, knowing that for all his own delight at the announcement, there would also be shudders of fear.

"What shall we do?" (Acts 2:37).

In preaching his Pentecost sermon, Peter reached for the repertoire of the psalmists: Psalm 16 and Psalm 110, as we have them in our Bibles. He knew that every song in the Psalter—songs of praise and thanksgiving, songs of petition and lament—was a melody either sung to or by Jesus—"this Jesus, delivered up according to the definite plan and foreknowledge of God [and] crucified and killed by the hands of lawless men" (Acts 2:23). In ways known to Peter and unknown to the writers of Holy Scripture, when the psalmists recorded their own complaints, they were also giving voice to God's own trouble.

We are not alone in the act of impolitic praying. God is himself a lamenter; he has raised his own anguished voice.

Psalm 22, as one example, gives voice to God's excruciating suffering from the cross: his physical anguish, his spiritual despair, his emotional turmoil. "My God, my God, why have you forsaken me?" David penned this psalm of lament, having no idea that Jesus would recite his mournful words as he drew his last breaths. The heavy boots of death were coming for God. Similarly, Psalm 69 picks up the details of the crucifixion, even the sour wine offered to Jesus for his thirst. "I looked for pity, but there was none and for comforters, but I found none." One might also imagine Jesus, on the night of his betrayal and arrest, praying the words of Psalm 42:

> I say to God, my rock:
> "Why have you forgotten me?
> Why do I go mourning
> because of the oppression of the enemy?"

God did not simply author the songs of lament: he sang them.

It is singular and shocking, this lamenting, dying God. As Dietrich Bonhoeffer argued, it's an oddly irreligious story, "a reversal of what the religious man expects from God."[5] We do not want God to falter or fail. But despite the stumbling block it would be to the Jews and the folly it would be to the Greeks, the apostle Paul made the crucifixion of Christ the lodestone of his preaching. He declared that he'd know nothing, preach nothing, exalt in nothing, rest in nothing but "Christ and him crucified" (1 Cor 2:2). Paul declared empathically that there is no gospel, no good news, no salvation apart from the cross—where the innocent suffers for the guilty and where mercy meets lament.

Without the breaking of God's body, there is no hope for God's broken world.

God's own lamenting, God's own suffering has proved that he does not remain indifferent to the anguish of the world, turning the dial for happier news than geopolitical crisis, natural disaster, local violence, tragic accident. God has practiced the truest form of compassion—suffering *with*. He is not a God of equanimity, made placid by his great ambivalence. John 1 tells us that God took up the liability of a body and pitched his tent of flesh in the middle of a Roman-occupied nation in the first century—which is just another way of saying that he descended to Baltimore and to Attawapiskat and to every dark corner of the world where death reigns.

▲ ● ■

God's suffering is not an answer necessarily, but it is a consolation. And even if the cross does not put to rest all the questions we have for the troubles we face, it assures us that God is fit to comfort. Like Job, we may not be able to make fundamental meaning of our suffering today: sexual abuse, rape, the loss of a child, widowhood, terminal illness. Although we can confidently believe that God "works all things according to the counsel of his will" (Eph 1:11), although we can attest to the greater holiness we will have at the hands of difficulty (Heb 12:10-11), although we can look expectantly forward, as Jesus did, beyond affliction to the joy set before us (Heb 12:2), life can still deeply hurt. Faith is not the same thing as stoicism.

Part of the practice of modest faith, in times of suffering, is relinquishing our right to answers. God has never promised to explain himself, but he has promised to stay near. I will never leave, he says; I will never forsake. I am the friend that sticks closer than your brother. Do not think me unmoved by your grief. These are the faithful assurances of God as we have them in Scripture, and there is even more hope available to those willing to search it out. But let's not be fooled to think that God has promised things like: it will get better, you'll soon see the purpose behind this pain, there's never more than you can handle. Often it does get better; often we do see purpose; always there is sufficient grace. But lament must practice the modest faith of finding sufficient that which God provides, even if, in seasons of great sorrow, it may not seem like enough.

Look to what Mary and Martha learned in the days following their brother Lazarus's death (Jn 11). Mysteriously, Jesus had stayed away after receiving news of Lazarus's illness. Inexplicably, he hadn't hurried to the bedside of his friend but tarried. When he finally arrives in Bethany, Martha meets him with an accusation. "Lord, if you had been here, my brother would not have died." When Jesus summons her sister, Mary, she parrots Martha's indignation. "Lord, if you had been here, my brother would not have died." The declaration masks a thousand unanswered questions. Why did you delay? Don't you care? How can we trust you fully? When the bottom falls out of life, this is what we all find ourselves wondering. And isn't it interesting that Jesus does not bring answers to the graveside? Instead, he brings tears. God weeps with the weeping. God laments with the lamenting. God suffers with the suffering. He is the man of sorrows of whom the prophet Isaiah spoke: "It was the will of the LORD to crush him; he has put him to grief" (Is 53:10). That's a song to sing—even an alleluia.

Man of Sorrows, what a name.
For the Son of God who came.
Ruined sinners to reclaim.
Hallelujah! What a Savior.[6]

God might have stayed in his nest on high; he might have chosen to remain deathless. A safer alternative to his own suffering might have been a handwritten letter to all the sufferers of the world, expressing his heartfelt condolences for their loss. And he would have meant it. But these are, of course, our human reactions to the suffering of others, which we often consider a contagion to avoid or a vulnerability to deny. If we indulge sympathy, we do so only at a safe distance.

But God, merciful and gracious, slow to anger and abounding in steadfast love, chose a different way to receive the laments of the world. Not dispassion and distance. Not practiced acceptance of dissolution and all things perishing. Instead, tears and even outrage. The cross is the site of his mournful fury at the falling, breaking, splintering effects of human sin on their own lives and the created order. Paradoxically, it is a wrath that he himself absorbs. As Fleming Rutledge writes, there is too little outrage in the world.

> Why has the gap between rich and poor become so huge? Why are so many mentally ill people slipping through the cracks? Why does gun violence continue to be a hallmark of American culture? Why are there so many innocent people on death row? Why are our prisons filled with such a preponderance of black and Hispanic men? Where's the outrage? . . . The biblical message is that the outrage is first of all in the heart of God.[7]

Lament tells us there are complaints worth raising, and God's suffering assures that someone hears.

▲ ● ■

On Sunday, October 1, 2017, Stephen Paddock opened fire from suite 32135 at the Mandalay Bay Hotel on the crowd below. He had stockpiled twenty-three firearms for his murderous acts, had calculated by hand the intentions of his devastation. A week after the tragedy, Las Vegas wedding photographer Mike Lichtenwalner realized that he had taken a photograph from the vista suite Paddock had booked and from which he had taken the lives of fifty-nine people, including his own. Lichtenwalner posted it on Facebook, and the *New Yorker* reposted it for an article they titled "Stephen Paddock's God's-eye View from His Las Vegas Hotel Room."[8]

> The cross is the site of his mournful fury at the falling, breaking, splintering effects of human sin on their own lives and the created order. Paradoxically, it is a wrath that he himself absorbs.

It is a paradox that a world bent on denying God has not scrubbed their language clean of him. Suite 32135.

Our sympathy and anger will not staunch the wounds of the world. We can divest ourselves of every privilege, but someone is still going to leave their four-year-old in the car to die in unexpected September heat. We can pray with the faith to move mountains, but someone is still going to learn that her little five-year-old's cancer has returned. We can work to right wrongs, but another black man is going to prison for a crime he didn't commit. And even though God will use every act of mustard seed faith for his glory and the world's good, we do not hope in the power of our agency or good will, but in the power of God's love to finally break death.

Most simply, lament means this: we groan aloud to God; we complain to the Big Cheese; we bring to the attention of the Creator and Sustainer of the universe all the unfinished business of the world. It is a paradox that we could be so bold as this, but that seems to be God's invitation: draw near to the throne of grace and receive mercy and help in times of *trouble*.

Over the last several years our friends have modeled the honest and vulnerable trust necessary for lament. Their business has faltered, and they have feared losing it. The husband admits, "I wake up in the morning and want immediately to crawl into the fetal position because the fear is so gripping." The wife describes the day she doesn't leave the house because she can't stop crying. "I used to read the psalms and wonder who they were for," she confesses. But for all the pain and perplexity, they keep rehearsing the story, keep bathing in the implausible truth that God is good all the time, all the time God is good, even as they pray painfully with the psalmist,

> My soul longs for your salvation;
> I hope in your word.
> My eyes long for your promise;
> I ask, "When will you comfort me?" (Ps 119:81-82)

One morning, my friend texts me a quote from Tim Keller, which she has run across in his devotional on the Psalms, *The Songs of Jesus*. "Suffering is unbearable if you aren't certain that God is with you and for you." She and her husband are learning to bear their suffering by rehearsing the promise of God's nearness. Maybe the mystery of suffering isn't only that this world could be so fragile; maybe it's also that God could be so close, bending his ear to the earth to let every grieving heart crawl inside and find rest. Not answers, but comfort. Not certainty, but trust. And perhaps this is enough to tide us over till the dawning of a new world when the heavy boots of death are sent straight to hell and everything fragile is made unbreakable again, where falling becomes rising and faith becomes sight.

A world where wonder is finally made worship.

QUESTIONS *for* REFLECTION
and DISCUSSION

1. What experiences of grief have taught you the unfortunate truth that this world is broken and fragile? Reflect on your own suffering as well as the suffering of others.

2. Do fears about the inevitable fragility of your world ever become crippling? How do you practice faith in those moments?

3. How comfortable are you with the idea that we can complain to God? What accounts for your relative comfort/discomfort?

4. What trouble are you facing presently that might warrant lament? How could lament help you to draw near to God? How could it clear the way for praise?

5. What troubles, besides your own, might you bring to God in the tradition of the weeping prophet? Think of your neighborhood, your city, even your nation.

6. How might the act of lament move you to compassionate action on behalf of your neighbor? How might you avoid relying on the power of your agency and instead trust the power of God for his rescue?

7. If God's suffering is not an answer to the why of human suffering, how can it be a consolation? How is it a consolation for you personally to know that God has not sought refuge from grief but entered it?

8. Who else needs to hear the good news of God's body, broken for them?

EPILOGUE

I'm home with mommy this summer!" Corrie exclaims as she waits to use the bathroom one Sunday morning.

Once a month, I supervise our children's ministry, greeting the kids as they run into the building, their parents breathless and harried, running behind them. I try remembering who is older—Sophia or Clara. I mistake Kinsley for Kiley. Months pass, and Hudson gets a sister. I blink, and Corrie matures into a dark-haired, dark-eyed kindergartner, her bangs cut with scissor-straight precision across her forehead.

As Corrie stands talking with me while waiting her turn for the bathroom, she abruptly becomes nostalgic, telling me about the crafts and stories and friends from the previous year. "I loved preschool!" she says fondly, as if remembering a distant past. I watch her bright eyes as she talks. I see that her world is saturated with possibility—that she, like every other child, drinks it in with wonder.

Wonder is not the condition of modern adult life; hurry is. We are famished for wonder, hungry for something other than haste and efficiency and productivity, something other than the fragmented attention we practice with our thumbs. I want more wonder in my life because the twenty-first-century mold, to which I must not conform, is that of the machine and interchangeable parts: I must endlessly speed up or get left behind, produce or find myself forgotten. But despite my tireless efforts to drive it hard and fast, my body is vulnerable. It wearies. It thirsts. It wills me to slow down just long enough to wonder, to marvel at the world as Corrie does, to recover the dignity of being human.

I know of no other way into wonder except by slowness, even if life is moving all of us at breakneck speed. The wonder-full life will not be gulped; it must be sipped. (I might hope that's been your experience of reading this book.) Wonder is, as Mary Szybist's poetry insists, the insistent impulse to "Look up!" It is, as poet David Whyte says, the hidden discipline of alertness. It was wondering that Mary had when the shepherds visited her and Joseph to recall the angelic pronouncement of God's glory in swaddling clothes. She "treasured up all these things, pondering them in her heart" (Lk 2:19). Wonder is the measured breathing we do below the surface of this world made and inhabited by God. In that eerie quiet of mystery, when we loiter, God offers us his gifts. As we give time for this kind of pause, we might just see the sham glory of the busy life.

In his Gospel, Matthew remarks on the wonder of the crowds as Jesus performed his astonishing miracles. "The crowd wondered, when they saw the mute speaking, the crippled healthy, the lame walking, and the blind seeing" (Mt 15:31). The hands of God repaired and restored, and the crowd *wondered. Wondered,* in the context of this passage, captures the many different facets of the word: that to wonder is to puzzle over, to struggle to understand, to marvel. It reminds us of the holy derivative of wonder: *wonderful,* which is the only fitting description for the kingdom of God coming to earth.

Like those crowds, I want to *wonder*: at the dawning of resur-rection, at the breaking of death. I want the kingdom coming to startle me today, to arrest my attention, to wake me from my preoccupied, numbed state of semi-consciousness. I want Jesus to walk the streets of my city, and I want to be there to drink in the sight of him.

Like Moses standing on Mount Horeb, wondering at "this great sight, why this bush is not burned," there is no way to near paradox except by wonder. Wonder helps us see the awesome God, a vision that cannot help but inspire a great bit of trembling and fear. When Isaiah saw God, he threatened to fall dead: "Woe is me! For I am lost; for I am a man of unclean lips, and I dwell in the midst of a people of unclean lips; for my eyes have seen the King, the LORD of hosts!" (Is 6:5).

Standing in the throne room of God, Isaiah met paradox and had wonder as a result. He wondered at God's promised stump of life and its "holy seed." After the land of Israel would be felled like a field of terebinths and oaks, after the promise of God would seem to be set to smoldering, God would deliver on hope in the unlikely form of a seed. God's words to Isaiah hearkened back to the promise at the very dawn of time, when God promised enmity between the "seed" of the woman and the "seed" of the serpent. In the Garden, after Adam and Eve's rebellion, God assured grace, speaking of the cross and his project of eternal salvation: "He [the "seed" of Eve] shall bruise your head, and you [the "seed" of the serpent] shall bruise his heel" (Gen 3:15).

God would not leave humanity and his world to ruin. He would rescue them, sending prophets to speak hard words to the people of God who, as Isaiah learned, would paradoxically "keep

on hearing" but fail to understand, "keep on seeing" but fail to
perceive. God's people would suffer tragedy and trauma, crying
out with lament, "How long, O LORD?" And God would answer
their cries in totally unexpected ways, paradoxically giving them
a king who "had no form or majesty that we should look at him,
and no beauty that we should desire him" (Is 53:2). God's King
would be acquainted not with triumph but grief, not with honor
but shame. This good news is a never-ending surprise, and it is a
paradox that the will of the Lord that crushes his servant is also
a promise of Christ's own consolation: "Out of the anguish of his
soul he shall see and be satisfied" (Is 53:11). How great a Father's
love that does not suit our expectations.

> **It is a paradox that the will of the Lord that crushes his servant is also a promise of Christ's own consolation.**

It's with greater wonder, which is to say
greater worship, that we must try to move
through this world voided of mystery.
Wonder is an invitation to cherish every
solid-brass truth that we can pass, like the
offering plate, in our Sunday liturgies—
and never to fear the tangles. It helps us
appreciate the knowable—and welcome that which is vast, un-
tamable, mysterious, and *awesome.* To wonder is to stand in the
towering shadow of God however frightened we are of our own
smallness. Like Moses, let us pause at the bushes that burn. Like
Thomas, let us bend for a closer look at Christ—even if, paradoxically, it's doubt that reaches to touch his side.

    Let us have certainty when it's available; let us have humility
when it's not. Let's remember that paradox, with its attendant
wonder, is its own way into the meekness of wisdom James describes in his letter. God is the author of *and,* and biblical faith

doesn't always have to be ugly, strident dogmatism, thistled with *either* and *or* and prickly to the point of drawing blood.

Mystery brings us to wonder, which is also to say the limits of our wits. But rather than our finitude bringing us to despair, paradox can cause us to praise. Indeed, when Paul refers to mystery, he often falls into doxology. "Now to him who is able to strengthen you according to my gospel and the preaching of Jesus Christ, according to the revelation of the mystery that was kept secret for long ages but has now been disclosed . . . to the only wise God be glory forevermore through Jesus Christ!" (Rom 16:25-27). Mystery will not leave you standing. It will force you to your knees. That's always the place we do our best wondering—and worshiping.

I told you that this book began in a counselor's office, with me asking the simple question: did I suffer the lying or sever the relationship? More than two years later, I can sadly report that the relationship continues to limp along, bearing the hard, unripe fruit of disappointment. I keep praying, keep persisting in the good and hard work of *and*. Nothing substantially changes. The family member I love continues to tell me lies, and I continue to feel uncertain about how to respond. I circle back to this bird with broken wings, sometimes more hopefully and sometimes less so. But truthfully, it is not always the place of despair and confusion it once was.

Like Job, I've come to more confidently believe the promise of "Deuteronomy 29:29 [which] essentially says, 'God reveals what he wants to—and be glad for it. But the secrets are all his.'"[1] I continue reading Scripture. I continue praying trusting prayers. I try giving up my desire for safe retreat into *either* and *or*; I surrender my need for control and clarity. I don't try to single-handedly repair the brokenness of this person's life, but neither do I abandon it. In short, I try becoming the child of the kingdom I am bidden to be. I sit squarely in the lap of Jesus and feel unapologetic to want the blessing for both of us.

In this book about paradox, I have taken us, however obliquely, by my own wondering through the major events of Christ's life: his birth, which is to say the incarnation; his public ministry, which is to say the proclamation of the kingdom; his death, which is to say the cross; and lament, which is to say Christ's resurrection and ascent. About the last act of this four-act surprise, until now I've said nothing. The ascension, as recorded by Luke in the book of Acts, is the moment that Jesus is assumed into heaven and takes his rightful place at the Father's right hand. The ascension, like all the other acts of the story, is a mystery, says N. T. Wright. The still-human Jesus is with us—yet absent at the same time. God is reigning—and will yet return to reign most fully. "To embrace the ascension is to heave a sigh of relief, to give up the struggle to be God (and with it the inevitable despair at our constant failure), and to enjoy our status as *creatures*: image-bearing creatures, but creatures nonetheless."[2] Because Jesus has ascended into heaven, we are not shaken, even when the world wrings us out with grief. There is a King. He is on the throne, and he will one day return to put every enemy under his feet. "O Israel, hope in the LORD from this time forth and forevermore" (Ps 131:3). Paradoxically, the story is both ended and hardly begun.

This past Advent, we sang this beautiful line of Gerald Moultrie's hymn: "Let all mortal flesh keep silence, and with fear and trembling stand."[3] I began learning how long a tradition, in Scripture, keeping silence has had. Job, having the audience with God he had long demanded, suddenly wisely decides to keep silence: "I lay my hand on my mouth" (Job 40:4). Moses tells the people of Israel to "keep silence" before their entry into the Promised Land. "Keep silence and hear, O Israel: this day you have become the people of the LORD your God" (Deut 27:9). King David, in many of his recorded psalms, insists that his soul waits in silence for God. He even commands it to do so: "For God alone, O my soul, wait in silence" (Ps 62:5).

We keep silence to hear God speak.

"Let All Mortal Flesh Keep Silence" points to the mystery of the incarnation, that "Christ our God to earth descendeth." But the hymn doesn't only insist on silence. It ends with the endless alleluias filling the world even now. "Alleluia, Alleluia, Alleluia, Lord Most High." Even here, there is paradox. The surprises in God's story beg us to keep silence—

And also to sing.

ACKNOWLEDGMENTS

*T*his is the third book that I've written in five years. (Incidentally, the first two, looked at more closely, touch on themes of paradox.) Truthfully, though my address has changed several times, my life substantially has not. As I've been keeping place in Toronto these past seven years, there are many people keeping me. I'm so grateful.

To my husband, Ryan: We have now officially spent more of our lives together than apart. You are an endless gift to me of wisdom, of humor, of partnership. I count our marriage as one visible expression of God's extravagant grace. Until death do us part, you are mine, and I am yours. I love you with all my heart.

To my children, Audrey, Nathan, Camille, Andrew, and Colin: I feel with great grief the shortening of days. (And yes, I did recently cry on the way home after I dropped you off for the first day of the school year.) One by one, you'll fly the nest. When you do and occasionally fall from flight, be reassured that I will never stop circling back. I love you with all my heart.

To my friends: I have needed you over dinner (Jill and Pete, David and Grace), on Voxer (Bronwyn, Aleah, Ashley, Laura), and in places far from Toronto (Jeni, Melissa, Kristy, Bethany). Thank you for listening, for praying, and for loving me in all my Enneagram one-ness.

To Dorothy Greco: Thank you for being an early reader and faithful critic. I know this book is the better because of your feedback.

To my pastors, present and past: I wouldn't be doing this work if you hadn't modeled for me a love for the Scriptures. Thank you for showing up, even when you didn't feel the passion of the sermon. Dan, you are an especially wise counselor, and I'm grateful you always pick up the phone when I call.

To the good folks at IVP, including my editor, Cindy Bunch, and my marketing director, Helen Lee: What a pleasure to have continued this partnership. Thank you for the good work you do in the world and the earnest care you provide for all your people. I have been so glad to be in this fold. Jeff Crosby, you are a gift to the many who know you, and I hope this book also finds room on your special shelf.

To Russ Ramsey: Thank you for generously offering your own words for the foreword of this book. I'm a great admirer of your work!

To the people of Grace Toronto Church: I owe you my best energies, so please hold me to that. Thanks for grounding me in the reality of God's coming kingdom. I love being a church in the city for the city with you.

Jesus: I don't pretend to know what it might be like to close my eyes to this world and awaken in the next. Clearly, this book is admission of my ignorance on a great many things. But I pray that when that day comes, the words of my life—written, spoken, lived—will have told the great story of your prodigal love. How I wish for alleluias to fill your beautiful, broken world.

NOTES

DEDICATION

Jonas McAnn is the fictional pastor featured in the epistolary novel by Winn Collier called *Love Big, Be Well* (Grand Rapids: Eerdmans, 2017).

INTRODUCTION

[1]"Who Was the Founder of Jehovah's Witnesses?," JW.org, accessed December 14, 2017, www.jw.org/en/jehovahs-witnesses/faq/founder.

[2]This is part of the *Oxford English Dictionary* definition as cited in Parker Palmer, *The Promise of Paradox* (San Francisco: Jossey-Bass, 2008), 6.

[3]Matthew Hutson, "Awesomeness Is Everything," *The Atlantic*, January-February 2017.

[4]Charles Taylor thoroughly treats this history in his *A Secular Age* (Cambridge, MA: Harvard University Press, 2007).

[5]The language of "sacramental tapestry" comes from Hans Boersma in *Heavenly Participation* (Grand Rapids: Eerdmans, 2011).

[6]Mike Cosper, *Recapturing the Wonder* (Downers Grove, IL: InterVarsity Press, 2017), chap. 1, Kindle.

[7]Boersma, *Heavenly Participation*, 2.

[8]G. K. Chesterton, *Orthodoxy* (Peabody, MA: Hendrickson, 2006), 81.

[9]Chesterton, *Orthodoxy*, 86.

[10]This is a lovely subtitle of a book by Marilyn McIntyre called *What's in a Phrase? Pausing Where Scriptures Gives You Pause.*

[11]Cosper, *Recapturing the Wonder*, chap. 1.

CHAPTER 1: THE GREAT I AND

[1]John Murray, *Collected Writings of John Murray*, vol. 2, *Systematic Theology* (Edinburgh: Banner of Truth, 1977), 133.

[2]Herman Bavinck, *Reformed Dogmatics* (Grand Rapids: Baker, 2006), 2:49.

[3]W. E. Vine, Merrill F. Unger, and William White, "Mystery," in *Vine's Complete Expository Dictionary of Old and New Testament Words* (Nashville: Nelson, 1996), 424.

[4]Isaiah Berlin, quoted in Jonathan Haidt, "Conclusion," in *The Righteous Mind* (New York: Random House, 2012), Kindle.

CHAPTER 2: ANNUNCIATIONS

[1]Mary Szybist, "To Gabriela at the Donkey Sanctuary," in *Incarnadine* (Minneapolis: Graywolf Press, 2013), 22.

[2]Szybist, "To Gabriela at the Donkey Sanctuary," 23.

[3]Karl Barth, quoted in Graham A. Cole, *The God Who Became Human* (Downers Grove, IL: IVP Academic, 2013), 144.

[4]Alexander Schmemann, *For the Life of the World* (Crestwood, NY: St. Vladimir's Seminary Press, 1973), 14.

[5]Schmemann, *For the Life of the World*, 16.

[6]Schmemann, *For the Life of the World*, 14.

CHAPTER 3: ONE WILD AND PRECIOUS LIFE

[1]I learned of Amanda Berry Smith in Karen Wright Marsh's *Vintage Sinners and Saints* (Downers Grove, IL: InterVarsity Press, 2017).

[2]Smith, quoted in Marsh, *Vintage Sinners and Saints*, 58.

[3]Athanasius, *On the Incarnation* (n.p.: Desmondous, 2013), 55.

[4]Athanasius, *Incarnation*, 17.

CHAPTER 4: A WORD ABOUT GLORY

[1]C. S. Lewis, *Mere Christianity*, in The Complete C. S. Lewis Signature Classics (New York: HarperCollins, 2012), 103.

[2]Collin Hansen, ed., *The New City Catechism* (Wheaton, IL: Crossway, 2017), 17.

[3]G. K. Chesterton, *Orthodoxy* (Peabody, MA: Hendrickson, 2006), 89.

[4]Chesterton, *Orthodoxy*, 93.

[5]Chesterton, *Orthodoxy*, 90.

[6]Chesterton, *Orthodoxy*, 90.

[7]Athanasius, *On the Incarnation* (n.p.: Desmondous, 2013), 16.

[8]Athanasius, *On the Incarnation*, 64.

[9]Athanasius, *On the Incarnation*, 67.

[10]Rankin Wilbourne, *Union with Christ* (Colorado Springs, CO: David C. Cook, 2016), 53.

CHAPTER 5: HIDING IN PLAIN SIGHT

[1]N. T. Wright, *How God Became King* (New York: HarperOne, 2012), chap. 11, Kindle.

[2]Graeme Goldsworthy, *Gospel and Kingdom* (Milton Keynes, UK: Paternoster, 2000), chap. 6, Kindle.

[3]In *How God Became King*, N. T. Wright argues that we read the Gospels as if we're reading the creeds. We focus on the virgin birth and the cross and resurrection, neglecting the importance of Jesus' public ministry in between.

[4]This is the analogy Dallas Willard uses to open his important book *Divine Conspiracy*.

[5]J. J. Niehuas, "Theophany," in *New International Dictionary of Old Testament Theology and Exegesis* 4, ed. W. A. VanGemeren (Grand Rapids: Zondervan, 1997).

[6]Graham A. Cole, *The God Who Became Human* (Downers Grove, IL: IVP Academic, 2013), 60.

[7]Wright, *How God Became King*, chap. 4.

CHAPTER 6: BLESSED ARE

[1]Dallas Willard, *Divine Conspiracy* (San Francisco: Harper, 1998), 122.

[2]Willard, *Divine Conspiracy*, 123.

[3]Alan Kreider, *The Patient Ferment of the Early Church* (Grand Rapids: Baker Academic, 2016), 137.

[4]Kreider, *Patient Ferment*, 137.

CHAPTER 7: BIRDS AND BARNS

[1]A. W. Tozer, quoted in Karen Marsh, *Vintage Sinners and Saints* (Downers Grove, IL: InterVarsity Press, 2017), 70.

[2]A. W. Tozer, *The Pursuit of God* (Camp Hill, PA: Christian Publications, 1982), 57.

[3]Ada Tozer, quoted in Marsh, *Vintage Sinners and Saints*, 73.

[4]Thérèse of Lisieux, quoted in Marsh, *Vintage Sinners and Saints*, 27.

CHAPTER 8: THE HIGH TREASON OF HALLELUJAH

[1]Noah Welland, "Evangelicals, Having Backed Trump, Find White House 'Front Door Is Open,'" *New York Times*, February 7, 2018, www.nytimes.com/2018/02/07/us/politics/trump-evangelicals-national-prayer-breakfast.html.

[2]N. T. Wright, *How God Became King* (New York: HarperOne, 2012), chap. 9, Kindle.

[3]A very important book on the congruence Jesus calls his people to, in terms of the way and the truth and the life of Jesus Christ, is Eugene Peterson, *The Jesus Way* (Grand Rapids: Eerdmans, 2007).

[4]Wright, *How God Became King*, chap. 9.

[5]Stoya, "Can There Be Good Porn?" *New York Times,* March 4, 2018 www.nytimes.com/2018/03/04/opinion/stoya-good-porn.html.

CHAPTER 9: FREE LUNCH

[1]Fleming Rutledge, *The Crucifixion* (Grand Rapids: Eerdmans, 2015), 20.

[2]Graeme Goldsworthy, *Gospel and Kingdom* (Milton Keynes, UK: Paternoster, 2000), chap. 7, Kindle.

[3]Rutledge, *Crucifixion*, 7.

[4]Rutledge, *Crucifixion*, 100.

[5]Rutledge, *Crucifixion*, 100.

[6]Eugene Peterson, *Practice Resurrection* (Grand Rapids: Eerdmans, 2010), 96.

[7]This was an idea from Richard Rohr, which I found referenced in Jennifer Grant, *When Did Everybody Else Get So Old?* (Harrisburg, VA: Herald Press, 2017).

[8]A. W. Tozer, *The Pursuit of God* (Camp Hill, PA: Christian Hill, 1982), 46.

CHAPTER 10: THE GRACIOUS COURSE OF RIGHTNESS

[1]Brandi Carlile, "Brandi Carlile on Practicing Forgiveness, Even When It's Hard," interview by Mary Louise Kelly, *All Things Considered*, National Public Radio, February 14, 2018, www.npr.org/2018/02/14/582454085 /brandi-carlile-on-practicing-forgiveness-even-when-its-hard.

[2]Dietrich Bonhoeffer, *The Cost of Discipleship* (London: SCM Press, 2001), chap. 1, Kindle.

[3]Alan Kreider, *The Patient Ferment of the Early Church* (Grand Rapids: Baker Academic, 2016), 150.

[4]Kreider, *Patient Ferment*, 155.

[5]Kreider, *Patient Ferment*, 182.

[6]Eric Andrew-Gee, "Hipsters of the Holy: How a Toronto Church Became a Hit with Young Believers," *Globe and Mail*, January 21, 2018, www.theglobe andmail.com/news/toronto/hipsters-of-the-holy-how-a-toronto-church -became-a-hit-with-youngbelievers/article37655616.

[7]William J. U. Philip, "The Law of Promise," *PT Media Papers* 3 (2003): 13.

[8]Philip, "Law of Promise," 6.

[9]Dallas Willard, *Divine Conspiracy* (San Francisco: Harper, 1998), 142.

CHAPTER 11: BIRDS AND BROKEN WINGS

[1]Leslie Leyland Fields, *Forgiving Our Fathers and Mothers* (Nashville: Thomas Nelson, 2014), 57.

[2]Fields, *Forgiving Our Fathers and Mothers*, 53.

[3]Charles Spurgeon, quoted in Tim Challies, "The Power of a Pleading Mother," *Challies* (blog), May 27, 2017, www.challies.com/articles/christian-men-and -their-godly-moms-charles-spurgeon.

[4]Winn Collier, *Love Big, Be Well* (Grand Rapids: Eerdmans, 2017), 30.

CHAPTER 12: THE EFFORTS OF GRACE

[1]Tertullian, quoted in Alan Kreider, *The Patient Ferment of the Early Church* (Grand Rapids: Baker Academic, 2016), 144.

[2]Dallas Willard, "Spiritual Formation in Christ: A Perspective on What It Is and How It Might Be Done," *Dallas Willard* (blog), accessed March 9, 2018, http://dwillard.org/articles/individual/spiritual-formation-in-christa -perspective-on-what-it-is-and-how-it-might-b.

[3]A. W. Tozer, *The Pursuit of God* (Camp Hill, PA: Christian Publications, 1982), 66-67.

[4]Tozer, *Pursuit of God*, 69.

[5]Tozer, *Pursuit of God*, 70-71.

CHAPTER 13: FLUENCY IN THE LOUD GROAN

[1]Sallie Tisdale, *Violation* (Portland, OR: Hawthorne Books, 2016), 303.

[2]Tisdale, *Violation*, 320.

[3]Tisdale, *Violation*, 227.

[4]Tisdale, *Violation*, 288.

[5]Tisdale, *Violation*, 314.

[6]Tisdale, *Violation*, 311.

[7]Tisdale, *Violation*, 94.

[8]Dan B. Allender and Tremper Longman III, *The Cry of the Soul* (Colorado Springs, CO: NavPress, 1994), 128.

[9]J. Todd Billings, *Rejoicing in Lament* (Grand Rapids: Brazos Press, 2015), 40.

[10]Ellen Davis, *Getting Involved with God* (Cambridge, MA: Cowley, 2001), 122.

[11]Davis, *Getting Involved with God*, 122.

[12]Much of this section is taken from Jen Pollock Michel, "Muddy River," *Image*, April 6, 2017, https://imagejournal.org/2017/04/06/muddy-river.

CHAPTER 14: COMPLAINTS DEPARTMENT

[1]Ellen Davis, *Getting Involved with God* (Cambridge, MA: Cowley, 2001), 121.

[2]Davis, *Getting Involved with God*, 15.

[3]Davis, *Getting Involved with God*, 21.

[4]This translation of Psalm 88:15, 18 is from Robert Alter's *The Book of Psalms* (New York: W. W. Norton, 2009).

[5]Walter Brueggeman, *Old Testament Theology: Essays on Structure, Theme and Text* (Minneapolis: Fortress, 1992), 29.

CHAPTER 15: UNFINISHED BUSINESS

[1]This is the subject of my first book, *Teach Us to Want.*

[2]J. Todd Billings, *Rejoicing in Lament* (Grand Rapids: Brazos Press, 2015), 45.

[3]Billings, *Rejoicing in Lament*, 38.

[4]W. E. B. DuBois, quoted in Josh Larsen, *Movies Are Prayers* (Downers Grove, IL: InterVarsity Press, 2017), 50-51.

[5]D. L. Mayfield, *Assimilate or Go Home* (New York: HarperOne, 2016), 77.

CHAPTER 16: A SUFFERING GOD

[1]In January 2016, the CBC reported the suicide of a ten-year-old aboriginal girl in northern Ontario.

[2]Ta-Nehisi Coates, *Between the World and Me* (New York: Spiegel and Grau, 2015), 17.

[3]Coates, *Between the World and Me*, 79.

[4]In *The Crucifixion* (Grand Rapids: Eerdmans, 2015), Fleming Rutledge draws out the parallels between Israel's important stories and the death of Christ.

[5]Dietrich Bonhoeffer, *Letters and Papers from Prison*, ed. Eberhard Bethge, enlarged ed. (New York: MacMillian, 1972), 360.

[6]P. P. Bliss, "Man of Sorrows! What a Name," 1875.

[7]Rutledge, *Crucifixion*, 129.

[8]Sarah Sentilles, "Stephen Paddock's God's-Eye View from His Las Vegas Hotel Room," *New Yorker*, October 6, 2017, www.newyorker.com/culture /annals-of-appearances/stephen-paddocks-gods-eye-view-from-his-mandalay -bay-hotel-room.

EPILOGUE

[1]Mike Cosper, *Recapturing the Wonder* (Downers Grove, IL: InterVarsity Press, 2016), chap. 6, Kindle.

[2]N. T. Wright, *Surprised by Hope* (New York: HarperCollins, 2008), chap. 7, Kindle.

[3]Gerald Moultrie, "Let All Mortal Flesh Keep Silence," 1864.

ABOUT THE AUTHOR

*J*en Pollock Michel is the award-winning author of *Teach Us to Want* and *Keeping Place*, both of which have been produced as original video series by RightNow Media in partnership with InterVarsity Press. Jen writes widely for print and digital publications and travels to speak at churches, conferences, and retreats. She's a member of Redbud Writers Guild. Jen holds a BA in French from Wheaton College and an MA in literature from Northwestern University. She is married to Ryan, and they have five school-age children. Their family attends Grace Toronto Church.

You can follow Jen on Twitter @jenpmichel, subscribe to her monthly newsletter at jenpollockmichel.com, or invite yourself for dinner the next time you're in Toronto.